MW00441342

There are few people in th[...]
Hilda has led as an indivi[...]
midst of few accommodat[...]
beyond hurdles is a testin..., ... remarkable strength in the
Lord, a testimony I hope many will read. I am so proud to recommend
this book.

—Kathryn Bryant Knudson, CEO of The Speak Foundation

Hilda's story is a gut-wrenching raw account of life with a disability
in Africa. But more than that, it is a moving account of God's ability
to transform lives. This is not a "tragedy to triumph" story, claiming
that God will change your circumstances if you ask enough. It is
a story of how God transforms a surrendered heart. Life with
a disability is hard on so many levels, but Hilda's story also
demonstrates the power of love and the aching beauty of trust. We
need more vulnerable stories like these, to show us as a society how
far we still have to go in affirming and valuing the *Imago Dei* in every
human being. Allow the Spirit of God to speak to you and move you
to act justly, love mercy, and walk humbly.

—Kim Kargbo, Founder & CEO of
Accessible Hope International

Hilda's incredible prose brings us up close and personal to the
struggles, mistreatment, and redemption that children living with
disabilities face every day. Her experience embodies the plight of
millions globally who are left behind by the world. I hope you pick up
the book and recommit your life to being a blessing to children and
young adults just like Hilda.

—Justin Narducci, CEO of CURE International
Children's Hospitals

This is not an ordinary inspirational story. This book will change you
from the inside. Hilda's is an empowering journey from relative
poverty and self-pity to achieving goals against all odds. It's not about

the fact that her body is impaired, it's not about pity or sympathy. This book shows disability is not inability.

—**Anne Wafula Strike, Ambassador for ADD International (Action on Disability and Development), Patron for Able Child Africa**

I laughed, I cried, I smiled, I felt like hugging Hilda for her bravery. I have never read a book that paints a picture of childhood in Cameroon so well, not to mention a child with an impairment struggling to cope, fall, and rise over and over again. Her inspiring journey has motivated my faith in God; it has stimulated a passion to do more for children with impairment in Cameroon who just want to live like other children. I want everybody to read it!

—**Agho T. Glory, Empowerment and Disability Inclusive Development (EDID) Program of Cameroon Baptist Convention Health Services**

Hilda's story transports us to the streets and into the homes and families of Cameroon. Trapped in a body of pain and disabling weakness from a young age, Hilda is driven to prove wrong those who dismiss her as worthless. Her confessions, unimaginable struggles, and bouts with hopelessness will echo in the hearts of many. But what if the faith that finds her could find you?

If anyone has ever dismissed you as worthless, if life's struggles seem overwhelming, if the future is dark and unknown, you will find someone who shares your tears and inspires your hope.

—**Rev. Christina L. Young, ELCA Pastor of "Fresh Bread" faith gathering, USA**

The Girl with Special Shoes tells the story of her struggle with muscular dystrophy such that you don't have to be suffering from any physical ailment to relate to it. Her resilience as she wrestles with existential issues provides guideposts for all travellers on the road of life. If you ever wonder anything about life's purpose, meaning, hope, and where God is in the midst of it all, this book is for you.

—Delphine M. Fanfon, Vision Bearer of
Me4real International, Cameroon

In a society where the disabled were considered cursed and a bad omen, Hilda was shunned, denied her rights, and constantly faced stumbling blocks. But no matter what, Hilda's tricycle went on, clinking and clanking forward toward her destiny. She shook the village, the city, and the nation, to become a symbol of pride and a trailblazer for many in Africa.

The more you read the book, the more you grasp that disability was not the enemy, but society's bias and ignorance. We can't afford to lose the potential of people who are disabled in body. The book is a testament of the power of a disabled body with a determined soul.

—Dr Segid Teklehaimanot, Psychiatrist trained
at Addis Ababa University, Ethiopia

You will suffer vicariously as Hilda retells moments of being neglected, cheated, abused, and forgotten. You will cling to hope with her as the unconditional love of her father consistently lifts her. It is fitting that God uses a lame child as a reminder to endure even the longest of journeys. My heart has been filled with gratitude and pointed to the day when there is no need for special shoes.

—Brandon Smith, Student Pastor at
The Well Community Church, USA

In breathtaking, authentic, and poignant moments, Hilda paints the battle between moving on and giving up, hope and hopelessness. God does not waste our pain. Hilda's special shoes are too big for me to wear, but they leave indelible prints and speak volumes throughout this side of eternity.

—Rev. Joel Ngoh, Former Lead Pastor at Hope Baptist Church,
Bamenda, and Mildred Tsangue, Therapist

Hilda's book is such an honest lament of what it is like to be disabled in a country where there is little help for the disabled. Worse, many people think disabilities are of the devil and avoid people with any kind of impairment. Her strong faith and true grit kept her going when most of us would have given up early on. I admire her. Even sitting in a wheelchair, she had complete control of a room full of children by her mere speaking than I ever had with full capabilities.

—**Sara Tanner, Founder of Supporting Native African Pastors**

I felt as though I accompanied Hilda through the highs and lows, through the support of family to deception, from special shoes to scary treatments by the witch doctor. Her book moved me to tears and left me wanting to hear more as God writes the rest of this amazing woman's story.

—**Jane Schmitz, veteran missionary in Africa,**
Association of Baptists for World Evangelism

Despite the many difficulties Hilda experienced, she overcame them with the strength of will, the support of her family, and the help of her friends. We in Egypt are so proud of her as a writer and artist who represents her country all over the world, especially in Africa.

—**Dr Nadia Elarabi, Executive Director of Alfan Alkhas**
Association in Egypt and Art Therapist

FOREWORD BY
JONI EARECKSON TADA

THE GIRL WITH SPECIAL SHOES

Miracles don't always look like you'd expect

HILDA BIH MULUH

The Girl with Special Shoes
Copyright © 2023 by Hilda Bih Muluh
All rights reserved. No part of this publication may be reproduced, distributed, or transmitted in any form or by any means, or stored in any database or retrieval system, without prior written permission from the publisher.

ISBN 13: 978-1-59452-859-0
ISBN: 1-59452-859-4

Published by Oasis International Ltd.

Oasis International is a ministry devoted to growing discipleship through publishing African voices.
- We *engage* Africa's most influential, most relevant, and best communicators for the sake of the gospel.
- We *cultivate* local and global partnerships in order to publish and distribute high-quality books and Bibles.
- We *create* contextual content that meets the specific needs of Africa, has the power to transform individuals and societies, and gives the church in Africa a global voice.

Oasis is: *Satisfying Africa's Thirst for God's Word.*
For more information, go to oasisinternational.com.

This book is a memoir. It reflects the author's present recollections of experiences over time. Occasionally, dialogue consistent with the character or nature of the person speaking has been supplemented. All persons within are actual individuals; there are no composite characters. The names of some individuals have been changed to respect their privacy. The author's views are her own. Places, people, and organizations mentioned are not intended in any way to be or imply an endorsement by Oasis.

The author and publisher have made every effort to ensure that the information in this book was correct at press time and disclaim any liability to any party for any loss, damage, or disruption caused by errors or omissions, whether such errors or omissions result from negligence, accident, or any other cause.

Unless otherwise indicated, Scripture quotations are from the Holy Bible, New International Version® Anglicized, NIV® Copyright © 1979, 1984, 2011 by Biblica, Inc.™ Used by permission of Hodder & Stoughton Ltd, a Hachette UK company. All rights reserved. 'NIV' is a registered trademark of Biblica. UK trademark number 1448790.

Scripture quotations marked (KJV) are taken from the Holy Bible, King James Version (Public Domain).

Cover design: Bupe Katungwa | Cover photo: Modesta Acha | Interior design: Natascha Olivier

Printed in India.

23 24 25 26 27 28 29 30 31 32 BPI 10 9 8 7 6 5 4 3 2 1

To all who have felt broken,
unheard, unseen.

You are special in God's eyes.

Table of Contents

Before You Begin

It was nearly 50 years ago that I shared my story in a book called *Joni*. It was a vivid and honest account of my struggle to embrace paralysis after the 1967 diving accident which completely altered my life. The book detailed not only the physical hardships of quadriplegia, but the spiritual ones – I found it nearly impossible to embrace God and his strange, hard will for my life.

For a long time, I could not understand why a good God would allow one of his children to suffer so much. But after years of digging through God's Word and earnestly praying, my heart began to soften. I did not so much find answers . . . I found *the* answer. I discovered that the God of the Bible was ecstasy beyond compare and that it was worth anything to be his friend. Even the harsh realities of complete and permanent paralysis. The *Joni* book detailed all this and much more.

When it was published in 1976, I prayed that God would use the *Joni* book to inspire and encourage other hurting people. But never did I dream that one day a high school girl in faraway Cameroon would pick up a copy. Hilda Bih Muluh read my story and immediately resonated with me, her "sister" on the other side of the world.

Even though our circumstances – and our disabilities – are very different, even though Hilda was raised in Africa and I was born in America, our stories feel so much alike. Both of us have suffered rejection, disappointment, and pain. I am convinced, however, that Hilda's experience with these problems goes far deeper. She grew up in a part of the world where disability is looked upon as a curse. Or a reason to stay hidden away in a dark back bedroom all your life. When Hilda was only a little girl, most people assumed she'd forever be a burden on her family and would never amount to anything.

You can see why I was thrilled when I learned how my story reached deep into Hilda's heart. But I cannot take credit for her life transformation. If our wheelchairs were parked next to each other right now, Hilda and I would agree, it's all about Jesus Christ and his amazing power to bring blessings out of brokenness. To bring about a far deeper healing than a physical one.

Hilda came to see a Christian's call to suffer is actually an outflow of God's love toward us. Like the apostle Paul, she viewed her disability as something that pushed her to lean more on God for his gifts of peace, strength, and contentment (2 Corinthians 1:9). She also found an extraordinary hope in the assurance that one day sorrow and sighing, pain and affliction will be forever gone (Isaiah 35:10).

Over time, my friend – yes, I consider Hilda a good friend – sensed that God was telling her to share her own story in a book. And I'm so glad that she responded to the Lord's prompting! There can never be too many stories about God's ability to bring triumph out of tragedy. Given the unique culture in West Africa, Hilda's journey from despair to delight in Christ is especially compelling. She overcame unfathomable obstacles that I know nothing about. And now? Her book *The Girl with Special Shoes* is ready to pick up where the *Joni* book left off, refreshing the hearts of a whole new generation of readers who long to understand God's purposes in suffering.

The humble volume you hold in your hands will unfold the most remarkable story of Hilda Bih Muluh. But it will also help you grasp how the tender love of God tempers the many trials that come to each of us, allowing only those things that accomplish his good plan. God takes no joy in human agony, whether suffering people live in California or Cameroon. In God's wisdom and love, every trial in a Christian's life is ordained from eternity past, custom-made for that believer's eternal good, even when it doesn't seem like it. Nothing happens by accident . . . not even the birth anomaly of a little girl born in Africa.

And so, I heartily commend to you *The Girl with Special Shoes*. Get to know my friend, Hilda. Listen and learn from this kind and gentle woman who has suffered through great distress . . . and you, too, will be "convinced that neither death nor life, neither angels nor demons, neither the present nor the future, nor any powers, neither height nor depth, nor anything else in all creation, will be able to separate us from the love of God that is in Christ Jesus our Lord" (Romans 8:38-39).

Joni Eareckson Tada
Joni and Friends International Disability Center
Agoura, California

The Walk to School

Half a kilometre would have been a minimal commute to school for most people. With my progressive muscle weakness, it was a vast gulf to conquer each day. Until I was 12, my delight in riding to school in Papa's taxi had been matched only by his delight in the grades I brought home. But then Papa's accident happened, and everything changed.

One day, the teacher left the class at 2:30 p.m. Students emptied the classroom in a matter of minutes. I could not carry myself and the books at the same time, so I put my books away slowly, stowing them in the open rectangular lockers of my backless wooden bench for my brother to pick up later.

It would be a while before the road was safe enough for me to attempt to walk home. After my father's accident, my family rented a little room half a kilometre from school so I could continue my education. My brother and cousins stayed there with me on weekdays.

The narrow stretch of tarmac could barely contain the volume of cars and thousands of students during peak traffic hours. With my very fragile mobility, I imagined I would be pushed over and swept away like a log in a fast-flowing current. So, I left the house much earlier and the school much later than everyone else.

Once the buzz outside died down, I picked up my bamboo cane, my faithful companion, tucked safely out of sight between the bench and the flaking wall. Using the wall for support, I moved outside to the veranda and leaned on a pillar.

A few students were left in the yard, either playing or sweeping the class for the following school day. I judged it safe to launch my long walk home. The little dusty stretch between my class and the tarmac was the trickiest part of my journey. As I took my first step, a gust blew dust into my face. I closed my eyes and turned my face, struggling to maintain balance.

A dangerous slope lay at the entrance to the school. To avoid it, I cut through the dining shed. It had a slope too, so I got down on all fours. The cane slipped out of my hand. As I reached to catch it, my foot slipped. I tumbled down the slant.

I sat back up. My knees and elbows were scraped and bruised. I blew on my scrapes to help the blood dry. I tried to dust myself off, but my feeble hands couldn't do much to restore my uniform to its sky blue and navy hue. At least the road was empty and I had the cover of twilight. I would be horrified to be seen looking like I had joined the birds in a dust bath.

I continued. *Other students go by without a care in the world. Lord, how can you deny me a very basic birthright like walking? Why do I have to be so different and so dependent?*

I imagined Jesus, walking on similar dusty roads, healing the sick and the lost. *Why don't you see my suffering and have mercy? Will you heal me too?*

I took a few more steps and stopped to rest. *How could you allow so much misfortune in one life? Why have you picked me out alone to bear such a heavy burden?*

I knew no one in my close circles who suffered as much as I did. I couldn't even think of anyone in other hospitals who were called to suffer more than I was. *What have I done wrong? Am I the worst sinner you know? Why else would you punish me like this? Not even Job in the Bible suffered as I do!*

I reached home after dark, five hours after school had closed.

The next morning, the 5 a.m. call to prayer from the mosque downtown was my alarm clock. I was exhausted. I wished I didn't have to go to school today. I wished I never had to go. I wished I didn't have to keep living to endure such torture. The imam's call to prayer was insistent. Finally, I got out of bed.

I took more time to bathe than usual. The icy cold water felt cruel as it trickled down my back. I wasted even more time getting dressed, somehow hoping that my reluctance would earn the pity of my siblings to give me a back ride to school.

My mother seemed to think my progressive disability was partially just being self-conscious about walking. She had insisted I walk part of the distance to ensure I did not lose all of my walking ability. It took me 10 times the amount of time others took to cover a very small portion of the distance. Then I would wait for a back ride from my brothers to take me the rest of the way.

Usually, my brothers got me to school before the flood of students. On other days, my assistants felt I could do a better job walking than usual. To punish my insolence, they would leave me on the road to teach me a lesson.

I dreaded the days when they came late or abandoned me. It meant I had to bear the piercing glares of every passing student, wondering why someone was crouching over a tiny Indian bamboo cane as if her very life depended on it.

My attempts to earn my brothers' pity backfired and I was instead sent off with scolding and warnings. I grabbed my cane and hit the road. My school bag would be brought by someone later. My tears blinded me as I took off into the dim light of the dawn, moving small baby steps and stopping to wipe my face with my free left hand.

Fine, I thought. I'll prove them wrong and make it to school on my own. I pushed myself to walk faster and almost fell on my face. I slowed down to my usual pace. Exhausted, I could only go a few metres. I could already see a few students trickling to school, an indication that I had left a bit later than usual. I managed to reach the trunk of a eucalyptus tree by the roadside and lean for support.

Thousands of students and others walked past me that early morning. Although my cane helped, I was unable to sustain this standing position for a long time, particularly in a bustling crowd. I was afraid of being trampled or falling. If I sprained my ankle, I would have to be taken home, and I hated the humiliation of this experience even more than the pain I would feel from falling.

As the only student with a disability among thousands on our vast campus, I envied others' ability to move around easily, their independence, their pride, their life. I felt like a helpless victim in an arena full of curious spectators who were not sure how to help. To them I was an enigma: beautiful, smart, looking like everyone else but unable to move like everyone else. At a time when disability was frowned upon as a curse in my society, I was trying to break the mould and live like a "normal" being. People's awkward reactions reflected a culture that believed in keeping its weak and vulnerable out of sight and out of the way. My parents were taking a bold step to send me to a regular school, and here I was paying the price of this experiment.

For the next hour or so, I hid my face near the tree and just sobbed.

I slouched in the clumsy position afoot the eucalyptus tree, clinging to my little bamboo friend for support. My legs must have been painfully cramping after the hour or two of standing on them, but I was too upset to notice. Eventually, I figured it was better to spend the rest of that day walking back home, since it was certain I could not make it on time to attend any class for the day.

A tap on my shoulder caused me to take my eyes off the ground. It was Bridget Moto. We had known each other from our primary school days. Bridget was one of my best friends. Her parents knew my parents, and we had exchanged home visits regularly.

She still bore the scars of burns that she had incurred as a result of a fire accident in their home three years back. During the months she spent in the hospital, I made sure that she was kept abreast with the schoolwork by copying down the notes twice and sending a copy to her parents to take to her in the hospital. We were fortunate to have made it to the same secondary school and to be in the same class, sitting on the same bench.

I had often comforted my friend when she went through a difficult time. Bridget had much to deal with in her own life – her parents' breakup, the challenge of covering the long distance to school daily, and taking care of siblings. I had encouraged my friend many times not to give up.

"What are you doing on the road?" my friend asked, half-chastening, half-surprised.

"I . . . My . . . " The tears started rolling again.

She looked at me intently, then she moved closer and held me up with both hands. I let go of my cane and collapsed onto her shoulder. She let me bawl.

She took up my head and asked, "Hilda, what is the matter? Did someone push you down?"

I shook my head, unable to mutter a word.

"Did your brother hurt you?"

Again, I shook my head and moaned.

"So, what happened? You've never cried like this before." She was right, I had never cried like this before her, not before anybody but God.

I pulled myself together. "Why does God hate me so much?" I said.

"How can you say that? God doesn't hate you. God loves us."

"Then why do I struggle so hard to do what is so easy for everyone else? I have been on this road for the past four hours, trying to cover a distance that everyone does in a few minutes. It's not fair." I shook my head in disapproval as I went on, "I'm trying the very best I can, but it's not enough to stop the suffering; nothing seems to work for me."

"It's OK. Let's go on to school," Bridget continued, gently stroking the cheek that was receiving fresh tears.

"By the time I reach school, I will only have to turn around and come straight home. So, I might as well save myself the trouble. I'll just go back home."

"You think I would leave you here by yourself? I'm not going to school without you." Bridget was adamant. A few moments of silence went by. I realized she meant what she said.

"Fine," I reluctantly agreed, "let's go to school."

I conceded to let her lift me on her back a few metres at a time. We made it to class halfway into the school day.

CHAPTER 1

The Gift of Family

My mother had married young and bore her first son before she was 18. For over four years, she faced prying in-laws who began to question her ability to produce more children. When I was born, there was great celebration in a dusty neighbourhood of Bamenda, the small town that served as the headquarters of the Northwest Region of Cameroon. My mother felt vindicated.

Our two-bedroom apartment was often thronged by family members both from Mami's and Papa's side of the family, some visiting and others staying for a long while. I felt significant and loved, even when Mami and Papa left us behind, the former for the Bamenda Main Market where she was a seamstress and the latter for I-knew-not-where with his yellow taxi. I always knew they would both come back – with treats for me and Achu Walters.

Achu Walters quickly filled the shoes of a big brother, helping and protecting me whenever he was not away playing with his friends. Our age difference meant we had few playing ideas to share, but he always kept a close eye on me and gave me the pet name "Jealous".

Mami returned from the market each day before dusk with food for the family for the day to find us bathed and waiting for a treat. Usually, it was *puff puff* (a fried dough snack) or fruit in season such as succulent mangoes, pears, or guavas.

I awaited Papa's treats even more. By the time he came back, everyone had gone to bed, except me. I hunkered in the foam Dunlop cushion of one of the few wooden chairs that constituted the main furniture in our tiny living room, struggling to stay awake, protesting vehemently at anyone or anything that threatened to take me to bed before my father's return. Papa ensured my wait was worth it. I received a real treat – chocolate (my favourite), biscuits, or candies, which I preserved jealously to show off the following day. Better than anything in the world, I went to bed on the warm shoulders of my hero.

Aunty Alice and Aunty Jane took care of us while our parents were gone. They were from our village, Pinyin, located some 20 kilometres from the urban centre. They lived with us so they could attend secondary school in Bamenda. I could tell they attended different schools from their distinct uniforms: an azure pleated skirt with a white sleeveless blouse and sandals for the one and a different tone of blue for the other. They left for school earlier than Mami left for the market and returned late in the afternoon to bathe us before Mami came back.

Like all the members of our jammed household, one was from Mami's side, the other from Papa's. I felt more akin to Aunty Jane, who was my Mami's little sister. She took me along when she went on visits around the neighbourhood and coaxed me to get my hair plaited. Aunty Alice and others might taunt or beat me for being naughty and snatching snacks, but Aunty Jane defended me.

Because the aunties went to school for most of the day, we needed reinforcement for the babysitting team. My great-grandmother, Manyu Deborah Zoh Neh completed the crèche. We called her Manyu Di, Manyu being her legitimate title for being the grandmother of twins and Di being short for Deborah.

Manyu Di was a feisty, no-nonsense caregiver, who looked nothing like her mysterious age. She seemed to be ahead of her time in her love for education and desire to speak the "white man's language". Her conversation, though in our native Pinyin language, never lacked a tinge of Pidgin English. She coined idiomatic sayings that have stayed alive right down to my generation.

She reminded anyone who cared to listen how beautiful she was in her youth. I asked about the lacerations on her face and her body. She said they were beauty marks gashed by her peers in her youth, a time when young men and women went about wearing only a little stringed covering to conceal vital lower parts. I could imagine children my age going around bare-bodied, but grown-ups? No way!

Manyu Di told us about life in colonial Cameroon under the Germans and later the British. Our part of the country, referred to as the Southern Cameroons, was a British Trusteeship until it voted for independence in 1961 and joined French-speaking *La République du Cameroun*. This explained our English expression and why we spoke Pidgin English everywhere except at home. Mami made sure that we stuck to our mother tongue while at home.

My great-grandmother's gifts also drew me to her. Every time she visited one of her numerous progeny strewn around Bamenda town, she brought back sweet yam, *egusi* pudding, and other delicacies. Manyu Di was the only one I knew who could tie up soup, runny or viscous, in banana leaves and carry it in her handbag without leaving a trace. When she returned, our watering mouths gathered to see what the banana leaf bundle would unveil while she called out names and dished out each one's portion.

For all her sweet charm, Manyu Di was a strict disciplinarian from whom my mother copied most of her own stringency.

"Pih, stop walking like that!" she chided, pointing to my feet as I tiptoed around her. I was about four years old, and I knew instantly there was trouble when Manyu Di chose to call me by my given name Pih, instead of one of the pet names she had a flair for coming up with.

She came over and tried to push my heels down. "Put your foot down like this." She stomped her foot on the dusty floor.

I would try and fail to walk properly according to her. She would give me a little slap on my arm or a nip on my cheek, thinking it was a childhood prank. I avoided her and limited my movement when around her, keeping my struggles to myself in hopes they would go away.

I loved to run and play around, and my difficulties were taking a toll on my four-year-old freedom. I had been the leader of our troupe of playmates, drawing the lines for *ntabalah* (hopscotch), making a ball from old pieces of cloth and nylon paper bags for "dodging" (our favourite), and dictating who got in or stayed out of the game. Unable to resist a tempting game with my mates, I would desperately attempt to play, run, and skip rope, but I kept falling. I was often disappointed and frustrated.

Manyu Di noticed something wrong when she had to pick me up more times than usual as I struggled to keep up with my peers in our childhood exploits. She watched as my hands couldn't hold on tight to anything, so I even dropped my food. One day, she saw me get into a fight with my peers. One of them slapped me. I was unable to fight back because my fingers were becoming limp and I could hardly stand on my own.

Years later, she told me, "For one who was a head taller and stronger than all her age-mates, I couldn't stand seeing you being beaten by others, even children younger than you. I did not understand why you would cry out in frustration instead of fighting back as I knew you to do. I would beat you, not knowing there was a storm coming."

How serious the storm would be, none of us had any idea.

CHAPTER 2

Daydreams and Nightmares

On days when walking felt difficult, I sat on the porch and watched the world go by. I dreamed of going to the Bamenda Main Market, where Mami's friends and relatives spoiled me with gifts when I visited. Or perhaps to the world of Grandma Tabitha's folk tales, where there were wise tortoises and singing birds, cheerful children clapping and dancing in circles. In that world, children and animals interacted without any barriers in language. These daydreams transported me from the present childhood games I was missing to a world of endless possibilities.

Most days, though, I was still able to go about with my friends. I bonded with Nahbila, the daughter of our closest neighbours, who was almost my age-mate. Nah and I kept little four-year-old secrets between us, guarding them jealously. One day we picked up a 25-franc coin from the street. Instead of handing it in, we bought two sweets, even though if our parents had found out we would have gotten a good spanking.

Another day, we agreed on what items to steal from our mothers' kitchens to use to make our game "play play" more realistic. "Play play" was when we impersonated the grown-ups. Lanky, domineering Nahbila played the role of the father, while I played the mother. If we succeeded to enlist other like-minded friends, we gave them the minor roles of children, helps, or drivers in our imaginary household.

"Wash that car quickly, I have to go out." Nah would feign her grown-up voice, crossing one leg over the other on her imaginary chair in the dust.

"Let me finish cooking first. Don't you see I'm busy in the kitchen?" I retorted, wiping non-existent sweat from my brow. I vigorously stirred the contents of the sardine tin on three pebbles, our fireside with no fire. Occasionally, my friends and I had real soup sweeteners, some salt, a flake of onion or two, some grains of rice or corn flour for *fufu*, items scavenged from our mothers' kitchens. On such days, I would scoop the "food" and place a drop in my palm. I would nod to indicate that it was OK or shake my head in disapproval, just like Mami.

When we were not playing in the yard, we ventured further and further from home to explore the neighbourhood. Our adventures might take us to the public tap at the junction, the water supply for the entire neighbourhood. Nah and I would fill our small plastic bottles with water to use the way we wanted at playtime. On other days, we followed the aroma of freshly baked bread to the newly opened bakery. Occasionally the bakery staff would offer us a bag of crusty overnight bread and pastries.

We visited a well-to-do family from our Musang Presbyterian Church down the road. They had a big house with carpeted floors and complicated chairs that were strictly out of reach for rough, dust-covered children like us. They cooked inside the house on a stove, unlike Mami, whose kitchen was a shack built with corrugated iron sheets behind our house. They served food at a dining table. When we neighbourhood children dropped by at mealtime, we were served food on a platter on the floor. I could swear that the food smelled and tasted different from being cooked on the stove.

At their house, I first came in close contact with a person of another race. We were enthralled by Laura and her matching doll, a white figurine with long blonde hair like Laura's. Her doll had big beautiful blue eyes that blinked, fingers and toes on her slender limbs, and even her very own dress! Where were such dolls made, looking like real human figures? We made our dolls from pieces of cloth Mami brought back from her workshop, wrapped around a stick. We attached the hairy roots of a grassy plant to the head to make it look feminine. Fascinated by the marvel, we took turns to touch Laura's doll, stroke Laura's sleek blonde hair, and sniff its sweet shampoo fragrance.

Mami could tell if we had played with Laura during the day from the questions I asked around the fireside as she prepared the evening meal. "Mami, what happens to someone's skin to wash off all the pigment?"

"Like whose?" she would ask, a little amused, as if she didn't know where I was heading.

"Like Laura's. Her body is white everywhere, even her hair!"

"That's the way God made her." Mami pushed a splinter of firewood into the fire. "You see how Neng and Nkeng look?" Neng and Nkeng were my cousins born with albinism.

"Yes, their body is white. But their hair is like my own." I touched the tips of my plaits.

"Mm-hmm. That's because they are related to you. Even then they are different. God makes everyone different. You, Achu, Tewah . . . ."

I paused, then asked, "What can I do to have my hair like Laura's?"

Surprised, she looked at me intently for a few seconds before responding, "Why would you want your hair to be like Laura's?"

"So that it can be long and it will not pain when they plait it," I muttered.

This answer seemed to satisfy her because she nodded before offering a response. "Your hair is beautiful like that. If they make it like Laura's, they will not be able to plait it anymore."

My mother's tone had changed from playful to serious, so I let the matter rest. It would not be the last time my mother and I would wrestle over changing or accepting my body's differences.

I was playing in the yard with my little sister one serene afternoon when Rose came.

Rose, another backup babysitter, was one of our neighbours up the road. Her imposing height belied a retarded mind. She had an endearing, gentle spirit and was willing to run errands for anyone, even little ones like us.

"Uncle Henry wants to see you," Rose said. "He says you should come alone."

Henry was the teenage son of our neighbours up the road, Rose's cousin. He often visited our house on Sunday afternoons to eat Mami's *achuh*, a Sunday delicacy, with many family members and friends. To us younger ones, he was known as Uncle Henry, the title we gave to men of a certain age that we could trust. Each time he visited, we ran into his arms expecting a little candy or biscuit for a treat.

The sun was in the centre of the sky. I could barely keep up with Rose's speed as we made the journey of close to 100 metres. The streets were calm, as everyone kept away from the sun's scorching heat. We met my summoner seated lazily on the veranda.

"Mom, how are you? You like biscuits, right?" Henry said, using one of my pet names. "Rose, go buy biscuits for Mom." Rose left obediently. "Mom, go and bring my shoes by the bed."

The bedroom was dark, which made me scared. I couldn't see any shoes. I turned to hurry out. Henry stood at the door, which startled me.

"I did not see the shoes, Uncle," I stuttered.

"Did you look well beside the bed?"

"Yes, Uncle."

"Go back and look under the bed," he said sternly.

As I bent over to search beneath the wooden bed, he walked over and stood by me. Thinking he had come to help look for the elusive shoes, I stood up. "Uncle . . . "

He grabbed me and put me on the bed. "Don't be afraid. I don't want to hurt you." My eyes widened and I moved back from him, further into the bed. He started unbuttoning his trousers.

I screamed. Maybe Rose or some passing stranger would hear me.

He pulled me to the edge of the bed. He cupped my mouth with one big hand, undressing himself with the other. With one of his strong hands occupied, I seized my moment. I squirmed from his hand and jumped down from the bed, screaming.

It took no effort for Henry to grab me and return me to the bed. He continued undressing. I took advantage of every interval to scream as hard as I could. I sobbed, praying earnestly in my heart for God to send someone to my rescue.

Rose appeared in the doorway. I had never been more grateful to see her.

Henry stopped and pretended nothing had happened. I slipped out of the doorway and went home.

From that point on, I tried my best to avoid him. Fortunately, we soon moved to another neighbourhood.

I did not tell anyone about the incident with Uncle Henry for many years. When I was older and more able to process it, I wondered what would have happened to me if Rose hadn't come soon enough. I heard many stories of other girls with disabilities who were not so lucky. I even learned later about a young girl whom Henry assaulted and impregnated.

I am playing in the yard with my friends when they come. Although it is daytime, I can see a dark veil behind these faceless creatures.

Instantly I'm alone. I start to run, but I cannot. I fall. I rise and fall again, reaching towards the house.

"Papa! Help me!" I shriek. No one comes.

"Mami! Aunty Jane! Anyone! Save me!" No one. I cry harder.

Long, murky, nefarious fingers bearing a rope reach down for me. They bind my hands and feet. They carry me away from the house, towards the dark veil. I twist my little body, trying to squirm free.

They are much too big and strong.

They approach the darkness.

I muster more strength and cry louder. "Papa! Don't let them take me away! I don't want to die. Please, please . . . "

"Pih, what is it?" Mami shook me violently. "Who is trying to take you away?"

I woke up, panting and sweating. The whole household was at my bedside like it was the last service being said for a dying soul. Still in a daze, I leapt and clung to Mami.

"Mami, please don't let them take me away."

"Look." She raised my tear-stricken face to look at her. "Who is taking you away?"

"They went there," I said, pointing to the wall as if the dark veil hung there.

"Shh." Mami enveloped me in her warm body. "Nobody is here now, only us. You see everyone?"

"Mmm," I mumbled. They returned to bed as she lulled me back to sleep in her arms.

This was my pattern in the early days of unanswered questions when everyone wondered at my increasing loss of coordination and my shrieks that woke the house. I often fell asleep in the bed I shared with my new little sister, Tewah Honourine, two years younger than me. I wondered why I woke up in my parents' bed. Papa said I was too scared to sleep after the nightmare.

For many years after I stopped having nightmares, my morbid fear of darkness remained. It became a sport for my siblings and cousins to lock me up in a room and turn off the lights or throw a blanket over my head.

CHAPTER 3

Houses of Healing

I knew Rose's appearance was a miracle. It was one of the first instances where I had called on God and seen him answer me so personally.

God was a part of our household every day as we grew up. We prayed at mealtimes and bedtime. We sang hymns often around the fireside. Papa read us stories from the black-covered Bible he kept beside his bed.

When Papa was in a very good mood, he narrated Bible stories or old-time stories of the Basel Mission. Its missionaries had brought the gospel to our part of the world back when Cameroon was a German colony, before the World War that changed our language. The Basel Mission had become the Presbyterian Church in Cameroon.

Somehow, however, we all seemed to feel God more on Sundays. I lived through each weekday looking forward to Sundays, when Papa, Mami, and everyone stayed away from work. The presence of the entire household made it a festive atmosphere as they all hurriedly took care of one thing or the other.

We woke up to the ricocheting sound of the pestle on the mortar as Mami pounded *achuh*, sometimes beginning as early as 4 a.m. *Achuh* was a staple meal of our region, enjoyed as much as the time and delicacy it took to cook.

Papa helped us get ready. Every week we dressed up in our bright princess gowns. Most children my age wore dresses bought the previous Christmas, aptly called *Christmas dress* even when worn after Christmas was long gone. We relished them every time we wore them, until another Christmas came around and tossed them off the top position. My sisters and I had the luxury of having a seamstress for a mother, so we had the extra privilege of a surprise fashionable dress every now and then, much to the envy of our age-mates.

Whenever Mami finished cooking early enough on Sunday morning, Papa would carry us in his yellow taxi to church, a moment I looked forward to all week. When she couldn't, we took the walk, past the junction with the public tap, across the road to Presbyterian Church Musang. In my struggle to walk along with others, I often fell on the dusty road, ruining not only my reputation but my much-cherished Sunday dress and socks.

Presbyterian Church Musang was where I was baptized as an eight-month-old baby. It was where Mami was a dedicated member of the Women's group, Christian Women's Fellowship, and the Alleluyah Choir. We loved to stand at the door of "Big Church" and watch Mami's choir and others animate the church service until the ushers sent us away to the children's section, "Small Church."

Being in "Small Church" was loads of fun too, especially when Na'a Tabitha taught us. She was older than the other Sunday school teachers, but not much taller than the children. Her genius was in composing pidgin English songs for every lesson and every occasion. These songs got us singing, dancing, and learning in Sunday school and throughout the week.

At offering time, she sang:

Jesus came, weti I go do eh?
Send hand for bag
Send hand for bag
Go gi'am for Jesus
Send hand for bag . . . [1]

We responded in unison with hand motions, bringing out our coins for the offering. On the Sundays when Na'a Tabitha taught, hardly anyone returned with their offering to buy *puff puff* on the way home or avoided "Small Church".

She had a rallying song to take us to church too:

Wuna came, wuna came
Wuna came we go for church
On Sunday, wuna came we go for church
Big man, small pikin, wuna came we go for church![2]

As she sang this, Na'a Tabitha marched military-style into the children's church building while the children followed along. I struggled with the hand motions and staying in line, but nothing dampened the momentary pleasure of joining Na'a Tabitha and my peers in singing at church.

As my mobility problems became more obvious, I began making frequent trips to the hospital. Aunty Jane accompanied me when Papa and Mami were busy. We waited our turn on wooden benches in the long corridors of the Bamenda General

---

1 What will I do when Jesus returns? / I will give him an offering.
2 Everybody come! Let's go to church / On Sundays, let's go to church / Adults, children, come, let's go to church!

Hospital, watching nurses parade in their white robes and starched crowns.

I gathered that this stone-walled building had something to do with making my legs and hands better. The bearded doctor closely examined them on every visit, asking my aunt questions. I spent the time taking in the smell of antiseptic and medical apparel in his office to use as evidence later to prove to my friends and siblings that I had been in a proper doctor's office. These hospital trips were another form of adventure to me. I returned with stories, treats, and other play gear for my friends.

On our way home, Aunty Jane and I would stop at Mami's tailoring shop at the Bamenda Main Market. My mother could scarcely wait for evening to find out the doctor's report. While she interrogated my aunt, I was busy underneath the sewing machine, collecting bits and pieces of cloth that would be useful for doll manufacturing later. Occasionally, I obtained permission to go a few shops down to visit our distant relatives. Aunty Francisca, who was actually a cousin to my mother, would give me delicacies and some coins from her provision shop. I got a generous wrap of yarn from another aunt who dealt in yarn and knit all sorts of baby gear. I returned smiling and richer, completely unfazed by what happened in the hospital.

But the numerous trips to the hospital did nothing to reverse my muscle weakness. Instead, I was developing talipes or clubfoot. Standing on my feet was becoming not only difficult but very painful. On bad days, I sat on the veranda, crying as I watched my friends play. I cried often, not so much from the helplessness of being unable to join them, but from sheer pain. My family and I were desperate for a solution.

If there was one family member who could execute desperate measures, it was my grandmother, Manyu Miriam. Like her mother, Manyu Di, and her daughter, my Mami, she was a stern disciplinarian. She had single-handedly raised nine children after being widowed at a young age and after her second husband left her. For many years, she traded in a male-dominated palm oil business with neighbouring villages. She used to trek from village to village to purchase palm oil. In her travels, my grandmother learned not only numerous local languages but also who were the most powerful "medicine men" in these places.

My grandmother frantically convinced my sceptical father to look beyond the "white man's medicine". She was certain it would not help much in my case. She had been informed, probably by one of the witch doctors, that there was more to my condition than met the eye. She would not rest until she confronted the dark forces of witchcraft purportedly crippling me. Thus, I began visiting the creepy huts and shrines of *doctas* in the various villages of our region.

During one visit, my grandmother guided me into a hazy room filled with a biting smell. She had brought the required items for my treatment, including a live black hen. The *docta* sat on a raffia mat close to the wall, talisman in one hand, cowries in the other. He threw the cowries repeatedly and read the prescriptions that he gave my grandmother. I sat very still and guarded on a little bamboo stool at the centre, trying to focus on the smoke-stained walls.

My chest tightened when the *docta* got up and came to me. Under his heavy moustache, he flashed teeth stained with kola nut. He was wearing a loose caftan from which I realized the biting perfume emanated.

Without addressing me, he called an assistant, who brought the black hen confined in a woven bamboo basket and a cup. My family knew my fear of live animals well; nobody with any good sense would frighten me with one. These strangers neither knew nor cared. A moan formed in my throat when the chicken was brought in, but I couldn't let it out. The assistant untied the hen's legs and handed it to the *docta*.

The *docta* warned me with a stern shaking finger, *"No shake, you hear?"*

My fear was quickly turning to tears. I turned and looked at grandma for help; she only said in our mother tongue, "Sit still and let him work on you, OK?" I had no defender.

I bowed my head, frozen in place. The *docta* towered over me like a priest ready to offer a sacrifice. Maybe I was the sacrifice. He placed the chicken on my head and both shoulders repeatedly while I tried hard to stay in place.

The ordeal ended after what seemed like an eternity. Before I could heave a sigh of relief, I was handed a black potion from the calabash. My grandma moved closer to make sure I didn't spill a drop. I squeezed my eyes shut and gulped it down. It was the most disgusting thing I had ever drunk.

The *docta* claimed these actions were needed for my cleansing because it had been revealed to him that I was an old witch posing as an innocent little girl. This was bad enough for a child struggling to find her place in the world, but I've heard of worse things happening to other children with disabilities accused of witchcraft. Some are taken to the riverside and, in the words of the *doctas*, "left to return to their world" – left to die.

We lived in one clinic for six months, in a small village called Kitiwum, nestled in a valley in Banso – farther from home than anywhere I had previously been taken. Mami was pregnant and could not come with me, so Manyu Miriam gave up everything to be my caregiver.

Every three days, the *docta* used a crude razor to cut into strategic parts of my body to put in an unknown potion. At first, I couldn't bear to see my blood oozing from the freshly cut wounds. Each stroke felt like a slash on my soul. My screams and squirms made matters worse. With time, I learned to sit still and weep within. The *docta* used the same rusted blade on all the patients he cut until it gave way. I can only thank the hand of Providence for keeping me from infection.

Looking back now, I find it hard to understand how a disillusioned *docta* could persuade a whole family to think that he could reverse clubfoot by constant laceration of the body. That they let me bear this painful ordeal for all the months was a testament to what lengths my family was willing to go to get treatment for me.

We were not alone in the clinic. This *docta*'s reputation was widespread, so patients came from far and near, living under the roofs thatched with palm fronds and sleeping on bamboo beds. They had little other than a mat thrown over to them. It was here that I was first exposed to the hideous reality of disease and poverty and the dent they can make on a hopeless soul.

Peter and Paul were identical twins seeking treatment for severe disability. They had been there so long that their mother had to resort to taking petty jobs from villagers to take care of them. While their mother left to work on farms, they were left on a mat in the yard the whole day. They curled on the mat, sometimes in their urine or faeces, until some fellow patient cleaned them up or their mother returned. Manyu Miriam and I shared our food with them.

My little heart melted with sorrow. *Why can't the docta give them a little mobility to be able to go around at least like me?* How pleasant it would have been if they could join Beri and me, my new friend a few years older than me.

Beri and I went to the farm in the early mornings to harvest *njama njama*, the staple vegetable eaten with corn *fufu* almost daily in Banso. One day in the field, I heard ominous sounds from a distance. In Banso land, a day seldom went by without drums, whistles, and gongs announcing a passing masquerade which we called *juju*.

I had heard tales of the most nefarious *juju* of the land, who could appear and disappear around their victim in the twinkle of an eye. They could outrun any mortal. Tongues were not allowed to tell what they did to their victims. No one could convince me that there were benign ones. Everything that bore a mask was an evil to be shunned.

Beri knew her way around the village pretty well and could distinguish the various masquerades just by hearing the music produced by gongs and drums from a distance. Beri told me, "Don't worry, the *juju* are headed elsewhere."

I could not stay still. I pleaded for us to go home before they got near, but she would not comply. I wondered what I would do if any of them appeared around me. The music got louder, and so did my plea for Beri to take me home. She only made good sport of it.

Feeling helpless, I burst into tears. That caught her attention, but it was too late. The *juju* were already within eyeshot.

Beri dropped the basket of vegetables, rushed over, and pulled me down. We both lay as low as we could in the furrows until they passed by. I do not recall ever going to that farm again.

My grandmother and I received occasional visitors from home while we were in Kitiwum, especially Papa. I was excited every time I saw a familiar face from Bamenda. It felt like a piece of home brought to us in a faraway place, and I made sure I made the most of the moment, enquiring about my parents, siblings, friends, and neighbours in quick succession. I was especially eager to hear about Mami's pregnancy. I had been asking Manyu Miriam constantly when we could go home to see my little brother or sister.

Someone knocked at the door one evening as my grandmother and I reclined. Between the flicker of the kerosene lantern and the fire, we could make out a face nearby. It was Uncle Simon from Bamenda, bearing a bag of goodies in his right hand. I waited for news of my newest sibling, but Uncle Simon seemed to be saving the good news for last. My grandmother insisted that it was rude for a child to interrupt grown-ups' discussions.

As he got up to leave, Uncle Simon said hesitantly, "Justine had a stillbirth."

Manyu Miriam ushered Uncle Simon out of the room for further questioning. When she had seen him off, she found me curled up close to the fire. I was staring into the flames and crying. She picked me up, cuddling me as she had done many times before. I went to sleep in her arms.

CHAPTER 4

Fountain of Knowledge

If my prolonged stay at the *docta*'s in Banso had been to "fix me" in time for the next school year, it had not worked. My limbs had not straightened, despite the *docta*'s boasts to make me better in little time. If anything, my feet could barely stay flat on the ground.

The *docta* insisted my treatment was not yet complete. Papa decided my treatment could continue from home. This entailed more bitter herbs to drink, foul-smelling objects to rub into my weakening muscles, and a small mysterious raffia bag.

The bag came with strict instructions not to peek or send a hand into it. Only I could ever touch it, and only when I had to drop a precious coin into it. This bag was asked to be hung, of all places, in a conspicuous spot in the living room. I spent many an afternoon fixated on this bag, wondering what hidden secrets the *docta* had kept within its entrails. Whenever my itching curiosity tempted me to look inside, I was deterred. I could almost hear the hoarse, frightening voice of the *docta* warning me: "*This one dey so,*" he had emphasized in Pidgin English, "*make no man no openam. If man try openam, weh, na ee know . . .*"[1]

---

1 "No one should ever open this bag. Anyone who dares open it should be ready for the consequences . . ."

Fear kept me from opening the mysterious bag for a few years. Eventually, my daring mother must have known that the powers were waning because she asked me to go into the bag and get coins to buy Maggi, a soup sweetener that we cooked nothing without. Nothing terrible happened, so I figured out how to steal into it for other personal errands. When we opened the bag some years later, great was our disappointment to see its contents: a dry leaf, a few cowries, and my few remaining coins. Fear doesn't need much to keep us bound.

I had returned from Banso with many bodily scars and interesting stories. My familiar friends clustered around each day as I told them about *fufu* and *njama njama*, the food that was cooked every blessed day there, the many places we went to, and the various types of coloured masquerades I had seen.

I was relieved to be home in time to begin school in September. I had crossed to the ripe age of five, and my right arm could now go over my head to touch the left ear. The grapevine held that this was the important criterion to determine if a child was of school-going age. My friends and I spent our days determining who was eligible or not by the ear test.

Walking and playing were becoming more difficult, but who cared about play anymore? I was going to school! At this point, our afternoon playtimes were spent finding out where each person was going to school.

I told Papa I wanted to go to school with Nah, but her Roman Catholic parents decided she would go to the Catholic School Azire, a distance from our home. Then I asked to follow Achu, my elder brother, to Presbyterian School Ntamulung, where he was a pupil. Again, distance was the main criterion to be considered for me, so I didn't argue when Papa decided the Baptist Primary School closest to home was my best option.

Fewer things made my father happier than education. He had never received more than a primary school education due to his family circumstances. However, he made sure he transmitted his love of education to us. He insisted on teaching my older brother and the many relatives that came through our home. Our evenings by the fireside were often spent singing one of Papa's songs or playing one of his games from his primary school days. Before we were ever old enough to go, we knew what to expect from school life: unending fun in singing, dancing, and games while we learned.

On the first day of school, Papa accompanied me on this journey to start drinking from the fountain of knowledge and wisdom. The smile that stayed on his face that September morning showed the joy and pride he felt within. I carried my slate and wore my uniform with dignity. It was grass green with white borders, tailor-made for me by my mother. She made sure she pleated it, as instructed by her five-year-old, "to look like my aunties' skirts".

Papa stayed with me for most of the morning. Children my age and older were drilled on how to stand on straight lines and march to the classroom. This was the most difficult part for me, but in the presence of my hero, I could brave any challenge. Our verdant regiment of a confused mini army marched to Class one, Pa Akenji's class.

Pa Akenji was a genial, potbellied, aged man. He always moved with a twig in hand to correct the naughty ones, but he seldom used it. He considered himself more like our father than our teacher, which commended him even more to us little ones. His patience with our rowdy lot was remarkable. He laughed and danced, teaching us through song and rhyme how to count and the letters of the alphabet.

I tried to sing and dance along with my classmates, but I kept falling. The mean kids named me *bend bend foot,* alluding to my clubbing feet, or *Eboa*, from a popular Cameroonian artist who walked with a gait. At home, my playmates called me names occasionally when we got mad at each other, but that didn't hurt nearly as much as having a stranger do the same. My classmates' taunts made me cry and long for the sanctuary of home. I was beginning to learn that the outside world could be very different, even hostile, to a little girl who looked and walked differently.

In the evenings, Mami often asked how school was going.

"That school is not nice, Mami. I will not go there anymore."

"Why?" she asked with concern in her eyes.

"Mami, they make fun of me. They insult my feet, and they laugh at me when I'm walking."

"Don't listen to them. They are jealous of your nice shoes and beautiful uniform." My parents must have known that I would face rejection as I ventured into a new world. They knew children can be mean towards someone different or with a disability. So, they had squeezed together their meagre resources to make me feel special. While everyone else depended on cheap second-hand shoes for school, mine were glossy, brand-new shoes that caught the attention of children and adults alike.

Mami used the tip of her wrapper to wipe my misty-eyed face as she drew me closer to herself. "When they get to know you, they will want to be your friends and play with you all the time. You hear me?"

"Hmmm," I sobbed in her wrapper.

This harsh encounter with the world of pupils could have crushed what little self-confidence I had, but it didn't. When parents love deeply, children can be made to believe in themselves and brave any hurdles.

Mami was right; it wasn't long before I started making friends in the new school. Most of them were casual friends, preferring to hang out at break time with their peers in the dusty schoolyard than stay with me. With the comments about my movement, I was beginning to gain self-consciousness, so I tried to keep a low profile, getting up to walk only when I absolutely had to. I watched my new mates play from a distance, imagining what Nah and my other friends would be doing under different skies. Feeling alone, I wondered why life had to be so cruel to separate us from each other, landing me among an aloof lot.

A few weeks into the school year, a cute little girl chose to sit with me rather than play with the others. Rosemary sat quietly the first day, stretching a hand to share her snack with me. I declined by shaking my head, remembering my mother's stern warning against receiving anything from people I didn't know. She came back the next day, and then the next.

Before long, Rosemary and I were inseparable. She came from a well-to-do family. We could tell by the beautiful car that dropped her off at school, her mouth-watering snacks, and the way her hair was plaited with extensions and held with shiny clips.

I shared with Rosemary my art of making dolls and made sure I brought along raw material from Mami's shop. Our dexterity sold our fame abroad, reversing the tide for me. Before I knew it, the other little girls started joining us for play at break time.

Because of Rosemary's friendship, I was fast becoming my ebullient self again, looking forward to school days. I was the centre of attention and I loved it. As our circle of friends grew wider, I took command, dishing out instructions on how the dolls would be made and who got to play with us or not.

The summer holidays came too soon. I was going to miss school, and especially Rosemary. We were consoled by the thought that we would meet again, this time as class two pupils. Throughout the three-month holiday, I kept asking those older than me to check the calendar on my behalf, counting the days until I would reunite with Rosemary. Unknown to us, fate had other plans.

CHAPTER 5

Strange New World

I enjoyed my first year of school so much that I was oblivious to my debilitating condition. But my parents noticed my gait had become slower and more painful. Mami would pick me up from school since she was a new mother again and was spending more time at home on her maternity leave. On the days when my feet hurt too much to walk on my own, she carried me on her back like a baby. By the end of the year, my legs had grown weaker, and my feet and ankles had become so tilted I could hardly place them down to walk.

Concerned, my parents sought other options for treatment. They learned about the Saint Joseph's Children and Adult Home (SAJOCAH). The lone rehabilitation centre that existed in our region, SAJOCAH was run by Roman Catholic Franciscan nuns and had a good reputation for handling difficult orthopaedic cases.

As soon as school was out, Mami and I hit the road again for SAJOCAH. It was situated in Bafut, a village about 25 kilometres from Bamenda. Papa's taxi rides sometimes led to Bafut, so we got up early that chilly morning to go along with him. Going on a road trip with both my parents was a rare privilege. It meant loads of fun and treats. Somehow the earth road did not seem so bumpy anymore. We arrived in Bafut before I could learn to say SAJOCAH.

We were greeted by a plain brick building, roofed with corrugated iron sheets, standing by the dusty roadside. A few people chatted here and there along the veranda. *Was this it?* It didn't seem like much in comparison to other hospitals I had been to. The noise grew wilder as we got closer. It sounded more like a raucous school compound filled with boisterous pupils than a hospital.

The door opened. Never before had I seen so many people with disabilities in one room. In Bamenda, I knew only of one man who walked with "sticks". Sylvester, our neighbour who was losing his sight, I unkindly chided to open his eyes wider, ignoring the log in my own eye with my onsetting impairment.

Here, I saw many children and a few grown-ups shod in strange apparel: some bound on bizarre machines, some tied to tables, some parading on sticks, and some pulling on weights and springs. I felt I was in a torture chamber. Their moans, laughs, and chatter created an irksome buzz in a hive I wanted no part of.

I cowered behind my mother's cotton wrapper as if to shield myself from the cruelty of this world. I didn't consider myself disabled and hoped never to be "one of them".[1] I was relieved when we were called into an adjoining room for consultation. It perplexes me to this day that I had such a visceral reaction to disability at an early age.

I reserved my questions for Mami in the crammed taxi on our way home. "What happened to that woman, Mami? She cannot get up and walk!"

"Which woman, Pih?"

<hr>

1 I generally use person-first language in this book to talk about people with disabilities, except when referring to negative attitudes that I or others held (e.g., poor, disabled girl).

"The one who was bending like this." I stooped over as best I could in the overloaded taxi, trying to show how the ageing woman had been holding her ankles and moving backwards slowly, very slowly. "Can she not get up and walk straight up?"

"Many people there cannot walk well. You saw the children wearing those iron shoes and some on sticks, didn't you?"

"But Mami, those ones who cannot walk are children, not grown-ups. How can a grown-up be unable to stand and walk on their own?"

My mother sighed and shrugged. Mami was an expert at nonverbal communication, and I knew not to press with my inquisitiveness when she had shown a sign. Perhaps her knowledge in this area was limited or else I could not assimilate her answer just yet. This unanswered question lingered on my mind for years. Ironically, my life experience would provide the explanation.

As our taxi galloped away, I was grateful I had been exposed to this weird world for only a brief while, grateful that I was going home, never again to return to such a place of despair.

How wrong I was. We seemed to have gone home simply to prepare ourselves for a longer stay. Before I knew it, Mami, Elvis Teneng (my new kid brother), and I went back. A little familiarity weathered the shock this time. I was told that SAJOCAH was a place to help elderly people and people with disabilities and that they might improve my feet. I became more excited to be there.

My mother said we would live with the other patients "for as long as my treatment lasted". We were taken to the dormitories, a little further from the first building. Each of the five dormitories was decorated with crucifixes and a poster of its patron saint. Our dormitory was named after Saint Jude. It was long and rectangular, with eight beds aligned on each side of the room and a passageway between the rows. Mami placed Elvis and me on one of the small iron beds and organized our belongings in a wooden locker by the side of the bed.

I soon began to make friends. I played with the other kids on the paved yard outside and on the iron bars that ran from the dormitories down to the physical therapy building. I discovered that the "iron shoes" so many kids wore as leg braces were called *callipers* and the "iron sticks" were called *crutches*. Even the grim equipment in the physical therapy room began to make some sense as I saw people exercising on it. Like school, there was singing, dancing, rhymes, and even real toys here. I cried at physical therapy and throughout the day, but Mami stayed by my side.

One thing I could not stand in SAJOCAH was the food. Cooked for a multitude, the food was flat. I threw up so often that my mother worried about how she would feed her starving child.

Enter Sister Norberta, the austere, brow-knitting, domineering, and stealthy nun who headed SAJOCAH. She was among the team of Cameroonians who had taken over from the missionaries. Her presence instilled fear in young and old, patients and staff alike. It was not uncommon to hear someone whisper in Pidgin English, *"Careful, Sister Nor di came,"* warning their neighbour at her arrival.

She had given strict orders for every patient to eat only what was served in SAJOCAH. No clandestine cooking was allowed under any circumstance within her premises. The penalty for breaking this rule was instant expulsion.

Most people complied, but my poor mother couldn't help it. She arranged to cook in the kitchen of a village family around the centre. This home-cooked food was way better than living on bread and biscuits and definitely better than SAJOCAH food.

One morning after physical therapy, Mami had gone to cook as usual with my brother on her back and me at her side. On our way back, Sister Norberta appeared. Mami held the incriminating pot of hot fried rice in a sturdy shopping bag in her right hand.

She had a split second to decide whether to throw the evidence in the bush.

I clung to Mami's wrapper, hiding from the cassock-clad, rosary-flaunting lady standing before us. My intrepid mother straightened up, "Sister, good morning."

"What is that in the bag?" Sister Norberta snorted.

"It's the children's food, Sister. They cannot eat the food from the kitchen here, Sister."

"I have told you that everybody eats the food from the refectory. If your children cannot eat the food cooked here, you should take them back home. If they are too good, then what are they doing here?" she barked as she moved away.

"OK, Sister." My mother feigned humility.

We exhaled in relief. My mother turned to look at me, with a wry smile on her face. Always beautiful, today my mother looked resplendent. She had stood up to the nun; my respect for her was growing. I learned that day that some challenges can only be overcome by facing them.

Now that I was older than six, my clubfeet could no longer be adjusted by stretching, twisting, and binding alone. We were to be in SAJOCAH for a short while, time enough to stretch and warm up my clubbing feet in preparation for minor surgery.

The surgery would be done in Njinikom Catholic Hospital, a partner hospital to SAJOCAH, located in a different village.

Each morning Mami would take us down to the physical therapy department for the day's exercises. I liked gliding along the shiny metal bars that ran from the dormitories down to the physical therapy building. I often challenged Mami to a race, which she always let me win.

I no longer saw the physical therapy room as a torture chamber. The buzz was part of SAJOCAH's vibrant community life. I had come to accept the people with diverse disabilities, who, like me, were there desperately seeking to ameliorate their situation. We just wanted to fit into a society that saw living with a disability as a curse.

But the main reason physical therapy had become less onerous for me was Sister Petra. Young and charming, Sister Petra radiated warm confidence that gripped my affection at this early age. Unlike Sister Norberta, she embodied love and acceptance. Her presence filled the sombre physical therapy room with light like a fairy godmother for us children. I felt privileged that our affection was mutual, giving me a chance to choose her to do my exercises often.

After a few weeks, it was time for us to move to Njinikom for surgery. Those who had been there said that Njinikom was a melancholy place to be but often came back better despite their scars. There were reports of limbs warped much worse than mine that had been straightened up. The patients embraced their new freedom, moving from crawling in the dirt to standing on their own, albeit with the aid of crutches and callipers. If these complicated cases of disability could be sorted, surely mine would be a breeze. For the first time, I dared to hope I would get better.

"Close your eyes, you won't feel anything." The tall male nurse beside my hospital bed removed my hand from the thigh area he wanted to clean for anaesthesia.

"Please! Please!" I cried. My fear of the needle was even more lethal than my fear of the *doctas*' rusty razor blades. I screamed harder and harder, looking to my mother on the other side of the bed for help. Instead, she conspired with the nurses, holding me down on the bed as they gave me the injection.

"Can you count from one to ten?" the nurse asked. The room became hazy before I finished. I awoke in a different bed in a different room.

Contrary to my great expectations, I came out of the operation room with much less freedom than I had had going in. Both limbs were cast up to my knees with plaster of Paris. I became a baby again, depending on my mother to be carried everywhere. When we returned to SAJOCAH a few days later, I watched with envy as other children played around freely, while I stayed shackled by my white casts.

Sister Petra noticed and took me into a little room for a chat. "Do you want to wear special shoes?"

"Yes, Sister." I stared, perplexed and helpless, at my casts.

"I will make you special plank shoes, OK? You will love them. You'll see." She touched my cheek in reassurance. She was enjoying the suspense her words created in me.

Another "Yes, Sister" was all I could muster as I watched her pick two small plank squares and pour some white powder into a bowl. A few moments later, my casts had been enhanced with heels. Thanks to Sister Petra's ingenuity, I could put my feet on the ground for the first time in weeks. She led me out by the hand to the physical therapy hall. Mami was surprised to see me walking!

Another September came. We had expected I would graduate from cast to callipers. Instead, the plaster was redone and left for much longer than we all anticipated. We were even asked to go home for a while before returning to SAJOCAH. I caught up with friends and loved ones, but I became the constant subject of curious eyes. My "special shoes" made it worse. I was relieved to escape their stares when the time came for us to return to SAJOCAH. This time, my grandmother came along with me instead of my mother – not a good sign of how long they expected my treatment to last.

I longed to see my friend Rosemary again since she was my only friend. But as she went on to class two, I was on the way back to the rehabilitation centre.

For months after I returned, I kept asking about Rosemary. When I had a chance to go to church, I would ask whether Rosemary was still in school. About a year later, I heard that she had suddenly gotten sick and passed away. *But she was so healthy! She had the perfect little girl's life! If anyone seemed sickly, it was me. How could death take away someone so nice?* It was the first time death had taken someone I knew, and it made a big impact on me.

CHAPTER 6

New Shoes

When I came home again, school was well into the mid-year. My movement had improved slightly, thanks to a pair of knee-length callipers I was given after the surgery. These leg braces were doubly inconvenient; they were very painful and so heavy that I could barely lift my legs to walk, but they promised to straighten out my clubbing feet.

While my feet were curling, wearing shoes had been a painful ordeal and I had to walk barefoot for some time. When my feet were getting straightened out, painful nodules had formed from walking on the wrong part of the foot. Mami picked shoes for me, mainly sandals with open sides, to allow the nodules to heal. I could think of nothing uglier than these colourful, cheap, plastic sandals with buckles on the back and front. I fought constantly with my mother about wearing them, sometimes preferring to go barefoot. I could hardly wait to wear "normal" shoes again, to fit in and live without everyone's prying eyes on me. This may have been what birthed my lifelong enchantment for good shoes!

So, I cared little about the new names my new "iron shoes" brought my way. I wore them with pride, waiting for the results to prove my critics wrong. I had Sister Petra's word that I would only have to wear them for a few months. To my mother's astonishment, I even volunteered to wear the callipers at night, separating from them only when I had to take a bath. I had been assured that in doing so, my legs would uncurl faster. A few months was a small price to pay for a lifetime of walking with good feet.

Another reason to fight for normalcy was that I didn't want to be like Nkeng. Nkeng was my second cousin who lived with albinism, a disparaging condition in my community. He also had cerebral palsy and had never walked a day in his life. He had been brought to SAJOCAH at a very young age. Then his mother left him and his other siblings in the care of stepmothers. Due to the instability at home, he had been left to grow up at SAJOCAH. Every time I saw him at SAJOCAH, I made sure I never got too close. *What if his reality rubbed off on me?* I resolved to never become such a burden that I would end up living in some undesirable centre in perpetuity.[1]

My family was moving to Alakuma, a more pristine part of Bamenda that was still partly untainted by urbanization. The slightly bigger house had an external room for the boys; my big brother and other cousins had grown too big to share the room with us. This meant that my sister Tewah and I had a room to ourselves. This room hatched and resolved many fights between us; it brought out our intense competitive natures.

---

1 After spending his childhood years in SAJOCAH, Nkeng was brought back to live in our village with his father. I reach out to him more often now. I'm grateful for the adults we have both grown into, even though I ponder sometimes what a difference would have been made for him, what opportunities he would have had, if only he had been blessed with a stable family as I was.

The members of our household had shifted. My two aunties had both contracted pregnancies as teenagers. Aunty Jane moved in with her husband to start her own family, while Aunty Alice returned with her baby to the village where her parents lived. After they left, other cousins came to live with us, some for academics and others to learn a trade in the urban centre, including my cousin Ferdinand.

Our new neighbourhood had many attractions to keep adventurous spirits alive. The stream was our most frequented spot. We fetched water there every day. Its main attraction was not the precious liquid but the exotic fruits and animals found along its banks. We learned the names of the fruits in Mankon, the language spoken by inhabitants of the village that once stood where the town of Bamenda was rapidly encroaching. *Atso'oh* was a slender reddish fruit and *ankop* was a scaly capsule with a large seed. I stubbornly followed other children on their fruit expeditions, ignoring my wiser older brother's advice to stay at home since I could not run.

One Sunday afternoon, I followed my brother and his friends to watch a movie at a distant relative's house, since we did not have a television at home.

I had first experienced television only a few years earlier. "Did you hear that the Awas have bought that thing called television?" It was the word on every tongue in the neighbourhood, grown-ups and children alike.

Someone who had been privileged to visit the proud owners the previous night would reply, "Did you know that the President has decided this or that?" There seemed to be a tacit agreement among the neighbours that one should desist after one or two visits, to make room for others. I went along with Mami and my brother one evening to see this new wonder. In the crammed little room, sitting on the cement floor with other children, we saw very faint black and white images on the tiny screen.

Between that and the conversations that followed, I grasped something to do with the President of the country, Paul Biya, who had recently taken over from long-serving Ahmadou Ahidjo.

Now in our new neighbourhood, action movies were the talk of Achu and his friends. Their dramatic re-enactments had a way of luring us into the plot of the movies they watched each Sunday. They liked to call each other "Jackie Chan", "Jimmy" for an Indian character, or "Commando" after Arnold Schwarzenegger's popular movie.

I decided to see for myself. I was excited to join them for my first action movie. Our noisy band chattered continually as we went. As we got closer to the house, the noise died down to a whisper. I tried to ask a question, but my brother put a finger on his lips. I was scared.

As we turned the corner, dogs started barking. Two dogs that were not on leashes ran towards our little band. Before I could turn around, the other band members had bolted into the nearby bush or run away at top speed. I screamed for my brother.

I fell and buried my head in the ground, praying the dogs would not smell me. Somehow, they passed me and pursued the kids who were running. Members of the household came to my rescue and called back the dogs. So shaken was I that my brother had to bring me back home instantly. We both missed the movie and I promised never to go along to watch movies again.

When September came around again, I was ready for school. I had blended into the new neighbourhood, made new friends, and was moving without callipers. My pace was greatly reduced, but I held on to the hope that since the surgery had helped my clubfeet, things would only get better from this point forward.

The closest primary school to our home, Catholic School Alakuma, was about a kilometre away. Achu enrolled in class five, I in class two, and Tewah in class one.

The school comprised three U-shaped buildings with grey cement walls, brightened somewhat by our turquoise uniforms. I was one among 66 pupils who sat under the tutelage of Aunty Therese. The respectful habit of seldom addressing elders without a prefix extended even to our teachers. They were referred to as Aunties and Uncles. The head teacher earned a "Mr" – a title we feared, not just due to his top position, but also due to his constantly stern demeanour around the campus.

Our teacher, Aunty Therese, epitomized all that we little girls wanted to be when we grew up: tall, slender, and beautiful. We agreed that she was the best dressed among the teacher folk, always making sure she melded the various parts of her outfit perfectly. We became little fashionistas ourselves, analysing how she dressed and emulating her in class and at home.

As I sat by the classroom window, my mind sometimes wandered back to my former school where I had met Rosemary. I wondered what my peers would be doing now in class three. I was jealous that they had moved a notch above me. I had been unfairly cheated of a whole school year and had to be vindicated. The thought jolted me out of my reverie back to the lesson. Right then I resolved to be the best in my class so I could skip at some point and be on par with my peers. This competitiveness and spiritedness were rare for a seven-year-old, but coupled with Papa's encouragement, I knew I had a chance.

When the first term ended, I came home sulking. My progress report booklet showed I was third in my class of 66. Being in the top three was good enough for everyone but me and my optimistic father.

"Mom," the name Papa called me when in good spirits, "you know you are not far from number one. Next term, if you work a little harder, you will be number one."

"Yes, Papa. What will you buy for me if I am number one?" My father loved and rewarded hard work, and I was determined to take all the carrots I could get from him. When the next term started, I had eyes on my father's prize and a reputation to protect. I never looked back.

As promised, Papa showered me with gifts every time I came first in the exams. I felt so privileged that I could name the gift I wanted from my father and get it. I began developing a sense of superiority over my siblings and others. I even disrespected older people around me and called them names, which landed me in trouble a few times.

To my father, I was the special little girl who had gone through too much already and could do no wrong. I bragged openly about being special because no one punished me for my bad behaviour, thinking they were protecting a disabled child.

Only my mother disciplined me whenever someone reported my bad behaviour to her. She forced me to exercise, assigned me chores she believed I could do, and didn't let my academic success get to my head. She let me know I was no different because of my disability. I compared Mami's tough love with my father's doling and began to feel she hated me. Later I realized without my mother's hard hand I would never have grown into a balanced and confident person able to thrive in an unfriendly society.

The following year in class three, I reasoned I could step up my demand for a reward by a notch. My father was ready to keep his promise and buy what I requested for Christmas if I came top of my class.

Feeling like a lady, I wanted shoes to match my status, a pair of glossy red ones with tiny heels. My drawing skills were often praised by those around me, so I used a crayon to depict my Christmas request to impress my father. Impressed he was; Papa bought a pair for me and another for Tewah. When we put on our shoes, we felt no other little girls in the world were as privileged as we were.

We didn't know of Santa Claus and didn't expect gifts from anyone but our parents. Christmas to us was about dressing our best and eating delicacies prepared for the festive day. Another highlight of our day was visiting relatives and friends who served more delicacies and gave us gifts. As children, we spent most of the year looking forward to these visits. They also required a great deal of trekking on roads steeped in the deep, omnipresent, ochre powder of the harmattan season. We never let distance, dust, or repetition of familiar activities spoil our joy and anticipation.

One evening over the three-stone fireside, I informed Mami of my Christmas itinerary: I planned to visit Aunty Francisca, Uncle Peter, and other relatives in different parts of town.

My mother saw cracks in my perfect Christmas plan. "Pih, I'm not sure you can walk a long distance with those high shoes. You know that from here to Aunty Francisca's takes you a long time, and Achu may not be there to help carry you."

"I can do it. I walk to school. It's not farther than our school," I insisted.

"My concern is those shoes." Turning to my father, Mami said, "I don't know why you bought her such shoes. See the way she already struggles to walk."

"I promised to give her what she wanted if she took first. I had to keep my promise, plus you know how Mom is if you don't give her what you promise," Papa defended himself good-naturedly.

"How many times have I told you not to give a child everything she wants?" Mami was always the one to consider all the facets of a matter. We all trusted her with the final say in family decisions; even Papa knew she was wiser. Our arguments were usually blithe and jocular, and we would let Mami draw them to a close.

Papa had adopted the alias "Peacemaker" from his youth, drawn from Matthew 5:9. It was emblazoned on his taxi. At home, he exemplified this through humility and a desire for reconciliation. It amused us when neighbours called us "Peacemaker's children". We would tease Papa often about this strange choice of name, but we copied these principles from Papa, which would be useful for all our lifetimes.

"Sometimes you give them what they insist on having so that they learn their lesson," Papa replied.

"Well, I hope she learns," Mami said. With that, the subject was changed and the evening rolled peaceably on as we savoured our fireside dinner.

Christmas morning came! With my fluffy pink gown and beautiful red shoes, I felt like Cinderella after a touch from the magic wand of the fairy godmother. So high-spirited was I that I refused to listen to the signals after taking a few steps in my cherished new shoes.

Tewah, Achu, and I took off after lunch for our first destination, Aunty Francisca's house. My sister strode along with ease, leading the way, but a few metres into our journey I started lagging behind. I struggled harder, but my feet were still recovering and the shoes hurt.

Unable to go on, I planted myself on the spot. Hot tears rolled down my cheeks. *These shoes were supposed to be my trophy for working hard and returning to normalcy. How could they humiliate me on a day like this?*

Somehow my all-knowing mother had convinced my older brother to accompany us girls. He came to my rescue and ended up carrying me for much of the trek to and from Aunty Francisca's. We never made it to the other places on our itinerary. It was a painful way of learning an important lesson. I was unique and maybe a little broken, but there was no point in me trying so hard to be like the other kids.

Various relatives including Aunty Jane,
my brother Achuh Walters, and me

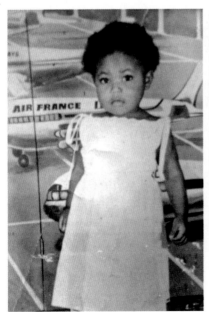

Me, at two, looking to
conquer the world

1986: Mami, Elvis and me
at SAJOCAH

Post-surgery, my first plaster of paris casts in Njinikom

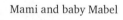

Mami and baby Mabel

Sunday morning with siblings
(L-R: Tewah, Baby Khan,
Britha, and me)

CHAPTER 7

A Big Girl

At eight years old, Mami thought I was old enough to start learning culinary skills. She entrusted me with the small kitchen tasks, like cooking *pap* for breakfast and boiling rice for the rest of my siblings. It felt like growing up in a real way. I enjoyed assisting her in preparing the spices for the soup. I peeled ginger and garlic and minced them with onion, waiting for her to put them in the pot.

When Mami's elder sister gifted me with a customized mortar and pestle, it felt like a rite of passage. I pounded alongside Mami on Sunday mornings before church, mimicking her every move. Although my end product turned out to be good enough only for my consumption, I beamed with pride and dreamed of becoming a strong woman like her someday. I couldn't wait to graduate to a bigger mortar as my skills improved and as I grew into womanhood. This was how young girls were groomed to run their own homes, a sacred ritual between mother and daughter.

But rather than get better at pounding in my mortar, I was losing grip of my pestle. The weakness was beginning to affect my fingers too, making them curl inwards even more. My kid sister was often called up to help me. It was humiliating to step back and watch her pound in my place. She handled the pestle with such ease. *What is making my hands so heavy?* It touched at the very core of who I was and who I hoped to become. I resented this new vulnerability deeply. I started to pick fights with my little sister and anyone who made mention of my disability.

My parents noticed the changes in my upper limbs and the lack of improvement in my walking. They took me back to SAJOCAH as soon as school was out. This time I didn't have to stay there. My feet were examined. The operation had successfully warded off the clubfoot. The new concern, Mami explained to the nun, was my hands.

Sister Petra asked me to hold different objects and squeeze her hand several times. She prescribed exercises for me to carry out at home. All of them were simple and harmless and could be done alone or with Mami's assistance.

Well, all but one. I lived each day during the holidays praying that the moment would never come when Mami would call me up. "Pih, come, it's time for exercise," Mami said.

I started crying. Mami held both my hands in her larger and stronger hands, squeezing them gently as if to reassure me before the torment.

"You see how this will help your fingers to be like this." She stretched out her fingers to show me. "When your hands are strong, you will do well in school and become a big woman and ride in a car, you hear?"

"Yes." I knew I could not resist my mother for too long. She entreated a child only long enough, after which she used force to get what she wanted.

"Show me your hands then." I stretched out my palms on a little wooden board and Mami wrapped a bandage around them to make sure they didn't curl up.

My hands would be left in this position for many hours, sometimes through the night. Of all the measures taken so far to make my limbs better, none had been so painful. Still, I knew Mami felt bad about inflicting me because she would keep a sweet or a biscuit by her side for me.

The bandaging done, I sat on the veranda, sobbing. I waited for the pain to kick in as I watched my friends and siblings play in the yard.

We followed this routine throughout the three-month holiday. The bandaging did very little to unbend my fingers. By this time, my parents had taken me everywhere, done everything they knew – even that which went against their creed – all to get a cure for me. The problem, it seemed, lay elsewhere – somewhere concealed from hospitals, witch doctors, and rehab homes. I went to bed each night begging God to take away my pain.

The focus of seeking treatment up to this point had been to stop my feet from curling in. Thanks to the surgery, that goal was partly successful. However, not much had been done to prevent the weakness that was now causing me to fall as I struggled to walk. Getting around on my feet was becoming agonizing.

My new baby sister Britha Ateh added to the four of us in 1988. Her arrival meant Mami was on maternity leave, so she could come to pick me up on her back each day and carry me home from school.

Some people made fun of my mother for carrying a big girl on her back. They felt that my parents should keep me away from school. They viewed my struggles to walk to school and the back rides I received from my family as a form of cruelty being inflicted on a weak, disabled child. Some of these people were family members who held the common belief that I was either cursed or the curse sent to destroy my parents, an omen that brought nothing but misfortune. Others were total strangers who were convinced that taking care of a child with a disability was a waste of time and resources. When they suggested Papa keep me at home or in an institution, they met his stubborn resolve: nothing would keep me away from school and family.

Mami eventually returned to her work as a seamstress, and I had to find other rides home. On good days, friends clustered around me as soon as the school bell rang at 2 p.m. One person took my stuffed school bag. Others offered their shoulders as crutches for me to lean on. We walked at a snail's pace, chattering and laughing together. When I got too tired to walk, the stronger ones carried me on their backs, and so we jumbled until they dropped me home and scampered off in their various directions.

On other days, I was left behind alone. One hot sunny afternoon, my friends were all carried away by juvenile preoccupations. The school compound was deserted but for a few senior pupils who were waiting for their late afternoon classes. I sat on the edge of my classroom veranda so they could lock up the classroom at the end of the school day. My eyes darted between the schoolyard and the road that made up the chasm that kept me from the comfort of home.

One classmate was still loitering around the classroom, Afor Maureen. I vaguely remembered when she had first come to school. Her uniform had been faded and patched, and she had held her few exercise books in her hand, without a bag. She had sat inconspicuously at the back of our overcrowded class.

Afor gathered up her courage and came up to me. "Are you waiting for somebody to take you home?"

"I'm waiting for the sun to go down before I start walking home."

"Let me help you."

I was taken aback by this gangly girl with bare feet. She laid aside her books and stooped for me to get on her back. I hesitated. *Can she lift me?*

What choice do I have? I got on. She rose with equine strength, picked up her books and mine, and we rode home. Afor carried me with an ease I had previously seen only in my brothers and parents. That day I learned to see beyond people's physical appearance.

For many months, Afor took on the responsibility of carrying me home daily without fail except for days when the school authorities sent her home early for not completing her school fees. When Mami understood this, she began to lay aside items of food and clothing for Afor to take when she brought me home. Afor's was one of the strong backs that have borne and keep bearing me through the journey of life.

CHAPTER 8

Miracles

Another girl who occasionally carried my bag was named Immaculate. She lived alone with her single mother. They attended the local Full Gospel church. These were the days when Pentecostalism was relatively new in my part of the world, so Immaculate, like others, was the subject of much taunting and derision in school. She stood out in her dress and her speech with a poise and maturity rare for her age. Consequently, she always stood alone, which is where we bonded.

Before walking me the rest of the distance home, Immaculate would sometimes invite me to her house. One afternoon, her mother was home, cooking a delicious, aromatic dish of rice and stew. She invited me to stay and eat.

As I sat in the living room, enjoying the fragrance from the kitchen, I noticed a poster taped to the wall. It showed the works wrought by a man named Reinhard Bonnke in his previous stops around Africa. Throngs of people enchanted by this charismatic man of God were depicted in frames each labelled with different locations. Colourful letters promised miracles, deliverance, blessings, etc.

A miracle! This was just what I needed, somebody to point me to a God who could heal my body. *All other attempts at*

getting better have proven futile because they have been human,
I reasoned. *If this next one is from God, then it must certainly
work.* I felt a sudden exhilaration: my miracle was imminent!

The famed evangelist and faith healer was coming to our
small town. Immaculate's mother asked if I would love to come
to the crusade to be healed. She told stories of miracles from
his crusades. I didn't need convincing. I had made up my mind
as soon as I saw the poster.

The crusade was scheduled for three days at the Bamenda
Municipal Stadium, a long way away from home for me. My
friend's mother seemed to be reading my mind because she
instantly offered to pick me up with her motorbike. All I needed
to do was inform my parents. This, I knew was going to be the
major hurdle.

Mami and Papa were stalwart Presbyterians, with a devotion
and commitment to their denomination that went without
saying. Baptized as a baby, I had often been told it was a sin to
join another denomination where I would be requested to be
baptized again. Papa seldom went to church, but he made sure
he read his Bible daily and taught his children to do the same.

He also taught us to resist any form of new teaching and
deeply disliked the newly arrived Pentecostal movement. Papa
had thrown out some people he met who were going from
door to door sharing the gospel. My family often mocked the
"born agains". Rumour had it that the members of these new
denominations spent time crying, doing absurdities, and using
the gospel ostensibly for sinister purposes like blood-drinking
and even witchcraft. This augured well for our superstitious
community. I was not naïve enough to think that my parents
would let me attend a crusade with such a "forbidden" group
without any resistance.

That evening, my family sat around the fireside as usual, eating our dinner and laughing at Papa's jokes and stories. All afternoon, I had played out scenarios, trying to decide how to break to my parents that I needed to go to a "born again" event.

"Papa, what would you do if I walked properly?" Everyone was quiet.

He gave it some thought before responding. "Well, that's what we have all been praying for."

"It is going to happen soon." There was certainty in my voice.

This last statement caught everyone's attention. The only sound in the kitchen was the crackling of the dying fire.

"I will go for the healing crusade that is coming up in the stadium," I announced.

"No way." My father's voice raised slightly. However, I knew that I stood a chance, given what desperate measures they had taken for my healing thus far. I chose to launch my next strategy on this soft spot.

"Papa, you also don't like witch doctors, but you have been taking me to many of them."

"It's your grandmother who insists on taking you there."

"Papa, if you let her take me there, you can also let her take me to this crusade."

"She's not here to take you, and you cannot go to such a place on your own."

"There is someone to take me." I was treading on slippery ground here.

His silence was indicative of an expected completion to the answer.

"My friend's mother. Please, Papa, let me attend."

"Does she have a car?"

"She has a motorbike," I quickly responded, hoping the disparity would not be too apparent.

My mother interjected, "Pih, you cannot sit on the motorbike; someone has to hold you." Mami had been listening silently the whole time.

She was right. I couldn't sit on a speeding motorcycle on my own, driving on our bumpy earth roads in Bamenda.

It took a lot more convincing and some tears, but a few days later, after school, I was wedged between my friend and her mother, on the way to the Bamenda Municipal Stadium to get healed. I had spent the last several days telling my friends that my life was about to change.

We got to the stadium as the sun was about to go to sleep. I had never been anywhere with so many people before. Some activity was already in progress on an elevated wooden platform at the centre of the dusty arena. Immaculate's mother joined the fray as a member of the organizing church. She entrusted me to the care of my friend.

I had heard all sorts of scary stories about large gatherings. I wished Mami had come with me. I clung to my brave friend as she led me to a pool of people with assorted disabilities. She told me to sit beside a ragged woman with intellectual disabilities. Then Immaculate excused herself, promising to come back later. I was all alone in a strange and dangerous place with a group of people I couldn't count on. My vagrant mind imagined me in a jungle, surrounded by invisible ominous animals, lurking in the darkness, waiting to strike . . .

A male voice on the loudspeaker brought me back to the crusade grounds. He welcomed us and invited us to pray. I looked around furtively and saw those around me were closing their eyes. I closed mine too – partially. I felt a sneaky pinch on my foot. I jolted and opened my eyes to see the shabby woman by my side flashing stained teeth in a smile. I couldn't wait for the prayer to end.

Choirs serenaded the crowd as we all waited for the evangelist to appear. The night grew dark, and the poor lighting meant we could hardly follow the action on the stage. The crowds were moving closer to the stage, becoming more hysterical. Those of us who couldn't push ourselves through guessed by the occasional shrieks that something major was happening. Then the powerful voice of the preacher came on the speakers. The healing time was over, and it was time for the message. A collection of offerings and it was time for my motorcycle ride home.

The commotion around the stage, Immaculate told me, was a result of various miracles that had occurred on the field. The miracle had eluded me and the pool of people with disabilities who surrounded me. *Why hadn't God come our way?* I pondered long into the night. *There were two more nights left. Maybe next time . . .*

Day two. Immaculate's mother took us on the motorcycle ride. Immaculate left me to wait with the other people with various ailments and disabilities. Still no miracle.

By the third day, I was beginning to wonder. I had but a very faint grasp of what faith was, but I knew that doubting had no part in it. I resolved to ward off the grains of doubt threatening to make their way through.

As my friend's mother took us to the stadium, I ignored the deafening noise of her bike and the bumps on the dusty road. I fixed my mind on my hope for my miracle all the way. I prayed God would show mercy and touch me and heal me while the "Man of God" was still in town.

When I reached my usual spot on the crusade grounds, a raucous crowd of young men stood not too far away. They faced the platform, making threats. Something about the atmosphere was ominous. I hoped my friend wouldn't leave, but she did.

As the activities began, the brassy crowd grew in number and tone. They accused the programme of deceiving the local population. It was impossible to hear the singing from the platform.

The mob began to throw stones and firebombs at the stage. Everyone scrambled to get out of the stadium.

What if one of the stones lands on me? I was a helpless little girl lost in a big wide world of tumult. If I tried to move in this crowd, it would be the death of me. Tears of despair ran down my face. *Immaculate, where are you?* Petrified, I stood on the spot and prayed – not for healing, but for protection.

Then Immaculate pulled me by the hand like the angels pulled Lot right before the brimstones rained down on Sodom. Somehow, we made our way to her mother waiting on the motorcycle. I thanked God for rescuing me. But I couldn't grasp why he hadn't healed me too.

CHAPTER 9

Higher Ground

Life returned to its normal pace after the crusade, albeit with more unanswered questions. Since I was rapidly losing mobility, I decided to invest my time in the things I could do well, instead of crying over the spilt milk of what I could not do.

Rather than envying my frisky able-bodied friends, I stayed indoors during the three-month summer holiday before my penultimate year of primary school. Papa possessed little more than the basic primary formal education, but over the years his love for knowledge had spurred him to study various subjects like French and literature. He had equipped a small personal library with volumes ranging from the classics to geography and even psychology. I invested long hours in the grubby pages of interesting volumes. Books opened to me a fantasy door of endless possibilities and a world of treasure that far surpassed anything I had imagined. I perused the Arabian Nights, seeing myself as an accomplice of ingenious Ali Baba, trapping the 40 thieves. My favourite was weaving my own story into the tale of Sinbad's adventures, going on an adventure with the audacious sailor each time he set sail.

My vocabulary grew with each passing day. While I read, I wrote down difficult words. Next to Papa's Bible, his *Oxford Advanced Learner's Dictionary* was out of bounds for me, so each evening he had to put up with my probing. He finally got weary of painstakingly checking the meaning of new words for me. He taught me how to use the dictionary and left me to my wits. What a promotion this was! I became the go-to person among my peers for difficult and new words, custodian of Papa's dictionary. Little did I know, this was laying a foundation for a future depending on the use of words.

"Can you pronounce this word?" I asked my peers with an air of superiority as they congregated on our veranda to hear one of the fables I had read. The word was *psychology*, which I had picked from *The Psychology Magazine*, an American-based magazine Papa had subscribed to years before. I picked it not so much because the topic of psychology interested me, but to ridicule my friends and to show off. The stories were spreading my fame and broadening my fan base. Before too long, I had more company than I could have had playing around the neighbourhood.

My great-grandmother, Manyu Di, occasionally visited us. In her unflattering style, she had begun to accuse my father's side of the family of having crippled her beautiful child because of jealousy. She considered my schooling and ability to read and narrate stories a victory over our enemies. Her admiration of my endeavours gave everything I did an added value. Whenever I wrote she stared in awe, coming close to lift my hands off the page and exclaim in our mother tongue, "Who would have thought such crippled fingers could carve in a book?" With that she would look to the sky, sigh, and carefully place down my hands in writing position.

When I knit, she marvelled even more. Drawing close to see my crocheting, she would clap her hands as women did traditionally to express amazement, then turn and address whoever was around. "This child of mine must be great. Have you seen where crippled fingers make dresses? They thought they had broken her but see the things she's doing with those bent fingers!" She turned to me. "My princess, you have to make one of these dresses for me so I can show my friends in the village what you can do."

I took my granny at her word and set to make a memorable gift for her. She believed that crippled fingers could be creative and helpful. This was all the fuel I needed. I was about to discover that setting out to prove a loved one right is a powerful key to success. I saved some francs and asked Mami to buy yarn from the Bamenda Main Market: a vivid red and white combination I knew my vivacious great-grandma would appreciate.

The yarn acquired, I began the ambitious journey of making a beautiful hat and matching little handbag for my dear great-grandma. My labour of love couldn't equal the years of love she had poured on me. Every twisting of the thread was a special reminder of her relentless sacrifice. My knitting speed was slow, compared to my peers, but I declined their help with this project. It was too personal, almost sacred to me. I met my goal of finishing before schools resumed for another year.

Many years later, when Manyu Di was almost confined to a bed, I asked if she remembered the little bag and hat I had made for her. My ailing granny took off her head scarf to reveal the hat underneath. It was dirty and discoloured. She had worn it ever since I made it and promised to keep it until she died.

When another school year came around, I was a year short of completing primary school. My father suggested I sit for the Common Entrance Exams – the official passage from primary to secondary school. I was ecstatic. This was my chance to catch up with my classmates who had gone ahead of me when I spent the year in the hospital. My teachers believed the exams would not be a challenge for me. I couldn't afford to betray Papa's trust, my teachers' trust, particularly that of Monsieur Jean-Paul.

Monsieur Jean-Paul, our lively and big-hearted French teacher, was loved by everybody because he was fond of buying trinkets and gifts for his best-performing students. He gave me my first-ever prize for excelling in a subject in school, a French textbook called *En passant le Moungo*.

I had another personal reason to choose him as my favourite. In my previous class, my school bag had become too heavy a burden to bear, either for the one carrying me home or for me on days when I had no help in sight. I got permission from the school authorities to leave my books in the classroom after school. One morning, I came to class to find the floor littered with shreds of paper from my books and an almost empty bag. Among the cherished books that the pilferer had done away with was *En passant le Moungo*.

Word quickly went around our little campus that my schoolbooks had been stolen. Pupil and teacher alike expressed dismay, wondering how a thief would stoop so low as to steal from a poor, helpless, disabled girl. When Monsieur Jean-Paul got the bad report, he gave me a new French textbook! French remained one of my favourite subjects throughout my school life because of him.

As I moved to class six, I had even more books, but I needed not worry about thieves anymore. Mami had come up with the brilliant idea to buy a vault-like box. I locked my belongings in it, leaving them in class. Each day I returned home with the key hanging like a precious jewel around my neck.

With this worry behind my back, other worries attempted to dim my excitement of being in class six. Preparing for final year exams entailed more commitment, more sacrifice, and more time than I was ever used to. Classes began as early as 6:30 a.m. and ended at 6:00 p.m.

To tackle the difficulty of getting me to school in the early mornings and surviving the long days, the entire family came together – my parents, siblings, cousins, and myself – to brainstorm on how to overcome this challenge. Achu had moved on to secondary school, joining my cousin Ferdinand, who attended the prestigious Government Bilingual High School Bamenda. Papa's driving job was taking him farther from Bamenda, our hometown. My sister Tewah, though younger, had joined my squad of mobility assistants. It was Mami's idea to spread the burden so it would be lighter for everyone to bear. She assigned each person a day to carry me to school Monday through Friday, according to their availability. The task of bringing me home from school fell to my brother, cousin Ferdinand, and another cousin, Anastasia, with whom I attended evening classes.

Normal school hours ran from 8:00 to 2:30 for classes five to seven. At 2:30, I came out of the class to sit in the sun on the cement floor, watching little figures flutter away and disappear into the horizon. Tewah closed school earlier, so she covered the two-kilometre trek from school to home and back. She brought me a delicious lunch pack Mami had prepared for me to eat before tackling evening classes.

The hour between the end of regular classes and evening classes was lonesome. I imagined the worst as I waited for my sister with the lunch pack. Stories of ghosts and apparitions of the dead were commonly recounted in our Catholic school environment. I was grateful our school did not have a cemetery like other Catholic schools around town. I was always relieved to see her little figure emerge from the horizon, growing larger and larger as she got closer to me.

Occasionally, my younger brother Elvis and even two-year-old Britha would come along with Tewah to keep me company until I returned to class. The entire family poured out their lives to ensure I was educated, everyone contributing a chip to my life edifice.

The speedy harmattan winds signalled Christmas break was coming. We children measured the intensity of the dry season by digging our heels into the dust to see how deep they could go. The season came with colds and coughs, crusted lips and heels, but we always enjoyed the celebratory atmosphere that came with Christmas preparations. Children skipped from one part of the neighbourhood to the other, collecting the rice, noodles, and other delicacies shared out by various social groups. Individuals often pooled together their resources in a mutual fund to buy items at Christmas, especially beef.

The cows that provided meat for Christmas were slaughtered not far from our homes. While other kids took up the sport of bothering the poor cattle tethered to trees, my fear of cows – and other animals – was numbing. As the cows' day of gloom got closer, usually a day or two before Christmas, they seemed to sense it. Every once in a while, we heard stories of someone having been gored by a cow in the neighbourhood. I made certain I steered clear of the dreaded beasts.

The day was December 23rd, and the frenzy of Christmas was at its apex. I had just taken my bath and sat on a bamboo stool in my usual spot on the veranda, facing the road to watch the busy world walk by. Everything seemed to be moving according to tradition. Kids and grown-ups chattered with excitement, carrying supplies on their heads back and forth. Everyone laboured so hard to cook the same things in the same large quantities every year, even though without refrigeration much of it would be thrown away.

A sudden commotion interrupted my thoughts. A swarm of people ran in one direction. *Probably just a rowdy mob of kids, pulling one of their pranks.* But adults were running as well, some of whom I had never seen running before. *What dreadful object is driving everybody berserk?*

A furious beast emerged from around the corner. My heart missed a beat. My first thought was to dash into the house. The door was metres away – still too wide a distance. The cow was getting closer. I could see the rope around its neck trailing in the dust. I ducked my head in my skirt, praying this would somehow make me invisible.

I sensed hoofs breeze by as the cow continued to breathe fury, pursuing its subjects. I waited until I was certain the storm was far gone. Once I mustered the courage to look up, I went straight into the house. Needless to say, my siblings and peers considered this the ultimate frisky adventure and made me the laughing stock that Christmas season.

I made it in the Common Entrance Exams with good grades, much to my father's delight. He never missed a chance to brag amongst his friends about my brilliant performance in school. Every time he had a visitor, my father would call me up to join them. Pretending he hadn't told them already, he would say, "Mom, tell them about your Common Entrance results." His childlike glee warmed my heart. He went on, "What secondary school are you considering going to?"

"PSS, Mankon," I chimed. Papa and I had rehearsed it many times over. I took this ordeal countless times. It was somewhat embarrassing and my siblings teased me, but I figured if it made Papa happy, it made me happy too.

The secondary school I was hoping to attend, Presbyterian Secondary School (PSS), Mankon, was an elitist mission boarding school known for producing some of the best results in the country. It was no secret that it was way out of the league of my straitened family. Papa would be making a tremendous sacrifice to send me there for school.

Mami started pointing out that my condition was not improving and I needed constant assistance, so I couldn't live on my own. She also asked if we could afford such huge sums of money for all the years of secondary school. Before long, everyone bought into Mami's idea and we settled for the next option, Government Bilingual High School, Bamenda. A reputable school in its own right, it was more affordable for necessitous families like mine. Both my older brother and cousin were already enrolled there and made a point of spreading its fame to us. When it came time to suit up in its two-shades-of-blue uniform, I did so with pride.

Again, Papa took me to secondary school on day one, along with my cousins Anastasia and Adeline. We had been to the rugged campus a few weeks prior for our interviews, exploring the many classrooms and dreaming of sitting on the dusty wooden benches. The school was nestled on a hill, giving a clear view of most of the city. It gave the impression that it was the high ground for knowledge-seeking.

My father dropped us off that morning, radiant in our uniforms, black shoes, and white socks. As soon as we reached school, my cousins rushed out of the Peugeot 504 car to join the rickety lines at the assembly. Unable to stand on my own, I moved to the closest classroom nearby and leaned against the wall. There was an address from someone I presumed was the principal, singing of the national anthem, announcements, and then the assembly was dismissed.

As students scurried in every direction, I watched, not sure which way to go. This school was not built with anybody with a disability in mind. Its jagged and rocky terrain made it impossible for me to get to most of the classrooms.

Papa had been to the administrative office and found out I was assigned to Form 1B, the very classroom against whose wall I was leaning. I couldn't tell whether to thank God or my father, but I was grateful for a classroom close to the road. Papa helped me struggle over a few steps to get into Form 1B.

In my first year in secondary school, I was exposed to children from varied backgrounds, some rich, others not so rich. We were approaching the teenage years, and little clusters of friendships formed. I was too poor to hang out with the rich ones, too shy to mingle with the talkative group, and too disabled to catch the eyes of the boys. I felt alone and neglected. My decreasing ability to walk around was limited even more by the sense of shame I felt for being different and my fear of being laughed at. I hated being called up to answer questions or write on the board in class. I came to class in the morning, never leaving until my father showed up at closing time to bring me home.

My resentment grew as I began to compare myself to others. I spent my lonely hours asking why God was cruel to me. God was not fair to give me the body I had, to place me in a poor family, in a poor country, and to refuse to heal me. This outlook rendered my school year miserable. I longed for the innocence and safety of home. My ingratitude blinded me so I stopped seeing the love and sacrifice that was being made on my behalf.

For the rest of this school year, my father dropped me off and picked me up from school. I looked forward to stepping out at closing every day to see him standing near the white Peugeot car, arms folded across his chest, waiting for me with a smile and a treat. His constant smile of approval was all I needed to wipe away the daily trials I had to face at school. So faithful was he that I began taking it for granted, feeling angry on days that the car broke down or he was impeded and I had to go home in a taxi.

I did not realize then that my whole family was paying an enormous price for me to stay in school. Papa's car was the only source of income for our household and yet he gave it up to take me to school daily. On weekends, he worked many extra hours transporting people to make some money to keep us going.

In my life, I have had to repent of ingratitude many times, especially when I consider how much others have sacrificed for me. While I was accusing God, my heavenly Father, of cruelty, he was showering me with love in the most amazing way through an uncommon earthly father. My father was God's gift of grace to me, providing just the love I needed. But I didn't appreciate it. Maybe it was time for a little reminder.

CHAPTER 10

Papa

It was a bright Sunday morning. We rose early to prepare for church service. Mami was pounding *achuh* while I bathed and dressed my youngest siblings. I was no longer able to walk the long distance to Presbyterian Church Musang, but I could help get everyone else ready to go. Mami called from the cooking quarters outside to see if we were ready. While she rounded off with the food, someone saw our uncle coming from the road.

Uncle Wilfred, my father's youngest brother, was a bus driver in Buea in the Southwest Region. On the rare occasions that he came to Bamenda, it was a great joy to us children. He never visited us empty-handed.

We gathered around to welcome him, but he was not carrying any gifts for us. He seemed shaken. He greeted us casually, moving towards the kitchen to see Mami. We all followed to hear what the news was.

"Pa has been in an accident."

Mami dropped the pestle she was holding.

Motor accidents were a common occurrence in my part of the country, particularly on the stretch of road that my father plied. Most of them were fatal. We had lost family members in some.

We all edged closer. Uncle Wilfred continued, "He has been brought to the Bamenda General Hospital. Yesterday they called me that he was in Tiko, so I went and took him." The Tiko-Douala Road was infamous for taking many lives. No one asked another question – we all feared the answer.

My mother rose without saying a word. She left the pounded cocoyam in the mortar and hurriedly changed into other clothes. My family's destination had instantly changed from church to hospital.

I could not walk so I could not go along. I sat on a chair by the door and watched as my family filed past, from the oldest to the youngest, following my uncle. An eerie calm filled the living room which had been a bustling junction a few minutes prior. I bowed my head as tears welled up in both eyes. *Is Papa dead? What if Uncle Wilfred is just breaking the news gently? No, he said Papa was brought from the accident site. He must still be alive. He has to be.* I clung to this glimmer of hope and prayed.

I would soon hear that other people had lost their lives in the accident and the car had been destroyed. But Papa's chair had given way with the impact of the crash, causing him to fall backwards and miraculously sparing his life. Papa almost lost his legs, but he was alive!

Family flocked in incessantly to form a strong web of support around us during the days after Papa's ordeal. I knew most of the circle around my parents' families, but I was surprised at how extended the branches of our family tree were. Distant cousins, grand-aunties, and grand-uncles, some so old they could barely walk, showed up to support Papa and us. Their presence lightened our mother's burden of looking after Papa in the hospital and taking care of the home at the same time. It opened our eyes to the rich heritage that was ours and assured us that we could always fall back on family when the going got tough.

Three months went by. Each day my family made several visits to the hospital, bringing food, warm water, and other necessities to Papa and the other people living with him in the hospital. Since Mami left very early for the hospital and only returned late at night, I stepped up as the oldest girl in the house, cooking, cleaning, and assigning chores to my siblings.

Others covered the two-kilometre distance each day on foot to the hospital, but it comprised a chasm that kept my father and me apart. There was now no car to take me out, and taxis seldom came into our neighbourhood due to the impassable roads.

Papa often sent me little gift packages with people returning from hospital visits. Other times, he sent notes encouraging me to keep my head in the books and to start preparing for the coming academic year. I told no one of my fear that his accident and absence would mean the end of my academic journey. I spent endless hours racking my brain for ways of continuing school without Papa to take me to school daily. I knew vocational training was off the list for me since I was irreversibly losing mobility.

My father had such high hopes for me that I was sure this hurdle was eating his mind more than mine. I wished I could talk directly with Papa. I longed to lay by his side as I always did, to thank him for sacrificing so much so I could be literate and to assure him I would keep going no matter what. I had read about those who got educated without ever stepping foot in a classroom. With the groundwork that had been laid already, I was convinced I could still build a firm academic future even if I never had a chance to go back to school.

Aunty Jane had moved back into town with her own family, which had now grown to include four kids. She knew I was closest to my father and understood his absence was taking a toll. She felt it was not fair for me to start another school year without seeing Papa. She suggested we pay more for a taxi to come as close to home as possible.

We picked a date for the hospital visit. I began preparations immediately. I picked one of my Christmas dresses for the occasion, a striped red and black gown. My hair was unkempt and overgrown after three months, but I washed and combed it to make it stylish. I didn't want my father to read from a shabby appearance that anything was wrong due to his absence.

With my aunt's assistance and frequent stops to rest, I made it from the taxi to the Bamenda Provincial Hospital's Accident Ward. The long rectangular hall had about 20 beds aligned opposite each other. A few of them had occupants. Papa's bed was at the far end.

I found him gaunt, dressed in a white pair of shorts and a shirt that seemed a little too big for his emaciated frame. He lay facing the wall.

"Papa," I called as I grabbed the edge of his bed.

He turned to look at us. His smile was faint and pitiful. I struggled to smile back, but tears welled up instead. I fought to contain them. This was meant to be a moment of rejoicing, not crying.

Papa struggled to sit up with my aunt's help. He stretched out his hand to greet me. I sat on the empty bed next to his and reached out with both hands. I could barely touch his hand. We both couldn't move our bodies to get to each other.

We exchanged pleasantries. Papa was curious to know how I was coping at home. He asked if I was excited to move to a new class. Papa always reminded me how going to secondary school meant I would be going a step further than he ever did.

I was eager to know how his accident happened. Ever one to tell stories, my father went into great detail recounting the incident that led to the accident. He was bedridden and crippled, but I was grateful he was alive.

I watched my father cheerfully accepting his fate. I rejoiced to see that his spirit had not been crushed. He spoke with such light-hearted humour that before too long we all were laughing together.

When he offered to share some food that had been brought to him, I gladly accepted, not minding the hospital setting. I couldn't afford to miss sharing another meal with my father. It felt like old times when I would wait for Papa to return from work so we could eat together.

I left the hospital that afternoon with a renewed spirit.

I took Papa at his word when he said he was returning home very soon and began preparing for the next school year. But he didn't come home. Instead, he moved to a hospital in another town, the Banso Baptist Hospital. He needed to get another surgery to save his knee and heal a festering wound.

In the three months he had spent in hospital, family members were growing weary of coming to our assistance. Only our closest family kept up their visits: Manyu Miriam, Manyu Di, and Papa's mother, Grandma Tabitha.

We began to feel the pinch of poverty. As the family had grown, Mami had left her sewing shop in the market to care for the home while Papa had fended for the family financially. His accident hit a hard blow to this well-oiled machine.

Without a source of income, Mami was left to run a home of seven children and extended family members, all on her own. Mami rented farmland to grow crops. My siblings joined her to sell boiled eggs, fritters, salt – anything she could quickly lay her hands on.

We had never lacked food before. Papa always made sure we were well fed and enjoyed delicacies from all the places his travels took him. Once the envy of other neighbourhood children, we now found ourselves craving a taste from their pots. We often went hungry all day, waiting for our mother to return from a far-off farm or the market to get us something to eat. A bag of food from the village or a plate from a kind neighbour was always a welcome relief.

Meanwhile, I continued to lose strength and mobility. Aunty Jane and her family lived barely a stone's throw from us. Now that she was a nursing student, we all looked up to her for an explanation for my mysterious condition. She guessed, like others, that my sedentary lifestyle and excess weight gain were to blame. Everyone believed this but me. Occasionally I argued that an inactive lifestyle would not affect my hands as well as my legs and that I had not put on that much weight.

Nobody cared what I thought though, so I had to subscribe to a daily exercise routine of walking around the house. Nothing was more daunting to me at this point than walking. I was falling more and often spraining my ankles. I pleaded for mercy, but my mother would show me none. I dreaded each early morning when she came in to wake me to go for the walk. I blamed God for letting it happen and I hated my mother for insisting that I go.

Some days, my aunt graciously offered her shoulder as my crutch. Other days, my mother accompanied me. Seeing how much time they spent helping me eventually convinced me that Mami's chastisement was not out of hatred but out of love. As the new school year approached and it seemed there may be hope of me continuing my education, I developed a new gusto to exercise.

In my father's absence, there was no way of bridging the distance from our home to school. The idea to rent a small room close to the school campus for me and my brothers sounded like the most plausible solution. From this close distance, I could attend school Monday through Friday, and return home at the weekend. My mother would give us some food for the rest of the week.

It was at that time that I had my fateful five-hour return trip from school, where I questioned God. And it was the next day that my friend Bridget rescued me, arriving halfway through the school day.

After arriving home that night, I lay on my Dunlop mattress on the cement floor, wishing the dawn would never come, hoping I never had to wake up to face another challenging day.

The imam's voice from the town mosque cried out to wake me up. I dragged the bucket of water along with the small stool I used for bathing outside. I struggled to keep the previous day's experience away from my mind, but it was impossible. I was not sure I could stand the previous day's humiliation one more time. I was aware of Achu's furtive glances as I dressed, ate my cold breakfast, and hit the road.

As I moved away from the house, I felt a presence behind me in the dark. I was too scared to look back. I had heard many ominous stories about the dark and prayed they would never happen to me. I kept moving.

"Wait!" came a voice from behind. It was the familiar voice of Achu. He caught up to me and stooped.

"Come, let me carry you to school." I handed him my bamboo cane without saying a word and followed his bidding.

A back ride from my brother that fateful morning saved me from much anguish. I made it to school earlier than everyone else. My fingers were numb from the cold harmattan morning, but I made it.

CHAPTER 11

Ghost Town

The year 1992 was also a historic year for my country Cameroon. Multiparty elections were organized amidst plenty of turmoil and confusion. The leading opposition party, the Social Democratic Front (SDF), created two years before, claimed victory in the polls. However, the ruling party, the Cameroon Peoples' Democratic Movement (CPDM), announced that they had won.

Our hometown, Bamenda, was the birthplace of the opposition party and the epicentre of the mayhem that ensued. Passions were rife; emotions were running high. The pangs of injustice and poverty were affecting many lives. They clamoured for change by rallying behind the new opposition leader.

The opposition declared "operation ghost town" in the city. These strikes, where schools and businesses closed and everyone stayed home, were a bid to pressure the government to yield to the people's demands and step down. A ghost town might last for two weeks. On Wednesdays, they would hold protest marches.

Mami went all in, joining the protests to help bring down a tyrannical government. She fuelled us with stories of how they had been repelled, marching from "Liberty Square" to the

Governor's Junction. Her optimism and excitement were visible every time she narrated how they had to dip their hankies in the dirty rainwater puddles in the streets to reduce the effect of the tear gas on their faces, or how they had devised ways of repelling the grenades that were thrown at them by quickly picking them up and throwing back at the soldiers. Still, lives were lost and limbs were severed.

The sound of gunshots was rampant around the city. When it got too serious, families started fleeing from the urban area back to their villages, where they felt more secure. My cousins Adeline and Anastasia fled with their families. We pleaded with our parents to take us back to the village, but they reassured us that the turmoil would subside soon.

Much later, I realized that the main deterrent for my family was me. My parents weighed the implausibility of carrying along a daughter with a disability for dozens of kilometres on foot against the danger of staying in the warring city and settled on the latter.

Calm returned after a few weeks, and we went back to school. Not everyone was convinced it was safe enough yet to return. Parents who could afford it sent their children to continue school elsewhere around the country. Those, like us, who had no other option, depended on the hope that things would turn around.

I was taken back to the room near the campus on a sombre Sunday evening to begin school the following day. With both my cousins away, I had only Achu to rely on and he was never one to be in one spot for too long. During these days of uncertainty, there were times when Achu was caught up on the other side of town. He would hear that there was shooting in town and couldn't make it back, so I had to spend one or more nights alone.

One time, Achu left for home and was unable to make it back. I spent a day without a caregiver, eating, or attending classes. On the second day, I held on, drinking lots of water to calm the persistent pangs of hunger and my groans of misery. I spent the entire day by the large wooden window of my room, hoping to hear the footsteps and panting that often announced my brother's arrival.

The day ended. No one had come by. As I bolted the window and door and got into bed, thoughts of dying went through my mind. I imagined what it would be like for someone to find my lifeless body in the lanky iron bed.

What if no one comes? What if no one ever sees my body? Would that mean my whole existence has been pointless? Part of me wished to sleep and never to wake up.

But another part of me wanted to keep living, to keep fighting, to keep hoping until the light of life's purpose dawned. *It can't all be pointless. There must be a purpose to my suffering, a reason for my life. It's not time to give up yet.* With this new resolve, my eyes scanned the room to see what tools I could use to keep going.

I had spent so much time in the scanty room that I had every detail etched in my memory, including the marks on the walls and nails on the plywood ceiling. Apart from the bed and the table, we had a rack made of cane where we stored food and plates, a tiny teal kerosene stove, and two soot-covered pots the floor. My few dresses and uniforms hung on a line that went across the bed, separating it from the reading table and chairs.

The only food items on the rack were a whole cabbage, a few raw plantains, and tomatoes Mami had sent along with me. Palm oil sat in an old container. Its brim had marks from mice who had doubtlessly found nothing better to feast on.

These would have been ingredients for a complete meal if my weak hands had been able to cut, shred, and grind without assistance. Still, I made up my mind to cook a meal the following day if my body and soul were to stay together.

I drifted into sleep that night with a silent prayer that perhaps God would see my predicament and grant the miracle of healing.

The day dawned with the call of a rooster and students bustling to school. The miracle had not come. I kept my window and door locked. I pushed books and papers to make room on the table, where I thought it would be easier to shred my cabbage in preparation for the cooking.

I had grossly underestimated the complex art of cabbage shredding. Try as I might, I could not do it. In frustration, I dropped the knife and resorted to using my teeth to pull out the chunks I could get. The same went for the tomatoes and plantains. The result was a peculiar meal that I would never have eaten under any other circumstance. It warded off the hunger until someone came along.

One afternoon as we sat in the classroom, the sweltering sunshine outside gave the school campus a certain calmness, the kind that causes one to daydream even as the teacher lectures away.

Bang! Bang! The gunshots were not far away. Ululation followed, calling people to assemble for a protest or go into lockdown. The classroom went berserk. Students grabbed their books, bags, and whatever else they could lay their hands on. Our teacher shouted for us to calm down. My classmates belted out, skipping benches or scaling windows to rush home before it was too late.

I watched helplessly. The teacher packed his belongings from his desk, paused long enough to glance in my direction, and then walked out too. Within a few minutes, the entire campus was deserted. I heard the last cars of teachers driving out.

Dazed and confused, I moved up to the door of the classroom. I still needed a plan to get home. I would have to walk back to my room on my own. I knew I couldn't make it in the heat of the sun. But it was too dangerous to wait until the sun went down. *It's better to die trying than to give up without trying.*

God, hasten my steps somehow! Grant me extra strength to get home before it gets too dangerous! I had read in the Bible how God intervened in impossible situations. This was a chance to see it happen in my own life. I stepped out homewards. I kept going, slowly, barely dragging myself along.

I had made it a few metres from the classroom when I saw a ghostly figure emerge on the solitary road. I imagined the worst and watched as he approached.

As he got closer, I could make out his clothes. It was a mason who was working on a building not far from the school. He had seen my brothers carry me home sometimes. When he noticed that other students were streaming down from school that day, he didn't see me among them, so he came to check on me. I couldn't afford to turn him down. He carried me as far as the entrance to our room.

The ghost town this time around lasted a few weeks. The government called a curfew in response. They would arrest or shoot people found wandering the streets if they suspected them to be sympathetic to the opposition. My wandering brother was away when the town closed up. Once more, I was caught on one side of the town, unable to unite with the rest of my family on the other side.

With no taxis in circulation, the only means of bringing me home was the famous back ride. But there were dangerous military checkpoints across Bamenda.

Uncle John finally dared to come get me. As I left the room on his back, I saw how Bamenda looked no different than the war zones we watched on TV. There were heavily armed soldiers in the various corners, burned car tires on the tarmac, charred vehicles and personal items strewn around the streets. To avoid falling into the dragnets of the soldiers, we had to improvise secret roads. Stops to rest and checkpoints did not help. It was the longest back ride I ever got – several hours. Uncle John and I got home sometime in the evening, to my mother's relief. This journey showed me the reality of the ghost town and how conflict affects the sick and the weak of any society.

CHAPTER 12

Independence

A fellow schoolmate had often seen me being carried on people's backs to school. Unknown to me or anyone in my family, he suggested that his father, who worked with the government social service, do something to help the situation.

Before I returned to school the following year, my father was contacted to bring me to the social welfare office in town. This was our first father-daughter outing since Papa had come home from the hospital. He now used a pair of wooden crutches to get around. After long hours of waiting and some paperwork, we returned home with my tricycle, the first ever mobility device I owned.

It was exhilarating to surrender my weight to its seat and be pushed around. The only problem was my hands couldn't push the pedals to propel the device. Papa was happy to assume the role of the driver on this first day. Pushing the tricycle from the back gave him some rest from his crutches. But I still had to grasp the pedals to steer, which was challenging enough. We were a curious pair of father and daughter, both with disabilities, one leading while the other belted out instructions from behind. "Hold tightly. Keep right, Mom!" Onlookers must have thought we looked like the blind leading the blind!

The tricycle gave me a freedom I had not had for years. I learned to pedal it, at least on flat surfaces. Achu showed me places that my disability had hindered me from visiting thus far: across streams and thick bushes, in the rain and the sun, to the homes of relatives close and distant. I had never realized my hometown was so extensive and interesting.

We revelled in my newfound independence, adventuring with careless abandon; but meanwhile, our mother still was struggling to cater for our large household. Papa held on to a glimmer of hope that the insurance company would compensate somewhat for his accident and we could go on with life as we knew it. He made constant trips to Yaoundé, my country's political capital, to no avail. As custodian of the household, Mami bore the brunt of the hard times. Despite her efforts, it was impossible to provide for us all with the daily demands of city life. Our daily food rations grew smaller and smaller.

Mami suggested the family move back to Pinyin, our village of origin, where we could easily farm our food, raise animals, fetch water, and collect firewood without having to pay money. We could also tap into the roots of the strong family tree. This suggestion did not please Papa, but with time he conceded. It was agreed that everyone would go except me, my older brother Achu, and my cousin Ferdinand who were in secondary school.

This meant I would be living on my own without parents to rely on. Many a teenage girl would have rejoiced at the prospect of such independence, the freedom to come and go, to do as they pleased. But I was no ordinary girl, and it was hard to accept. *If only I had a strong body!* I dreamed of all I could have done to help my mother and save my family from these trials. I had read stories of ordinary people who defied untold odds and accomplished unbelievable feats when they believed in themselves. They reminded me to push for more. During that season, I read many a story of resilience that gave me the strength to survive.

I spent weekdays in my tiny room around school and weekends at Aunty Jane's house with my cousins. All younger than me, they welcomed me like a bigger sister into their den. Soon a different cousin, Anastasia, moved into my room to be my assistant during the week as well. She was in the same class as me, and we had been buddies since primary school.

The tricycle attracted such attention on our school campus that I never lacked someone to push me along. After school on Friday afternoons, I had an army of volunteers marching behind me. Cousins, friends, and neighbours assembled in force, taking turns to push my tricycle as we marched onward to Aunty Jane's house for the weekend.

With the strong troop to support me, I was almost oblivious to onlookers' stares of derision and pity along the way. On some days, we arrived home drenched from the rain but rejoicing all the same. I missed my family terribly, but the love and support from this wonderful crew made my transition as seamless as possible.

Aunty Jane made sure I was comfortable, often going out of her way to do so. Her house was big and newly built. It had modern facilities that we never had in our own home, like an internal bathroom so I didn't have to struggle bathing in the open. Her husband, an avid reader, had a rich collection of books and magazines that enchanted me. His *Reader's Digest* magazines were a reservoir of knowledge and wisdom. From one of the stories, I gleaned a phrase that would be my mantra for years to come: "Bloom where you are planted." Watching television and lots of movies made the time away from family fly by.

Before I knew it, I was 16 and in the final year of secondary school, preparing for the General Certificate of Education Ordinary Levels. If I passed these exams, I would go on to two years of high school to do Advanced Levels, and maybe someday university.

This was the time when young boys and girls started considering future dreams. Because Papa had always broadcasted my academic results, my family and friends often asked me what I planned to be in the future. In my first year in secondary school, I had read in a textbook about the first female pilot in Africa. I set my eyes to the sky, ready to prove everyone wrong by following in her footsteps. I yielded to the wise counsel of others when I realized that my weakened limbs could hardly carry me along on this path to the skies.

For a while, I entertained the thought of becoming a doctor. My father's dream was for me to become a lawyer. I wasn't sure about that, but my gnawing desire to stand out persisted. One of my teachers, Mr Che, introduced me to journalism. I began to consider this too, partly because I had started admiring the presenters I watched on television back in Aunty Jane's house and partly because I was coming to the realization that my weak limbs would not augur well with practical sciences.

In Form 4, I was assigned to a class that was predominantly science oriented. Our academic system used students' performance to determine what they should study. It dawned on me that without focusing on the arts subjects, I would be losing hold of an attainable dream. I, therefore, set out to convince the school authorities to relocate me to an arts class. The confusion that ensued almost cost me a whole academic year.

After several letters to the principal's office, persistence paid off. I was transferred to the desired class – Form 5A. I celebrated this victory by promising myself I would work extremely hard and succeed against all odds. It helped that I had developed a love for reading, because not only did I study the literature texts we were assigned in very little time, but I also started excelling in the new subjects in my new class.

CHAPTER 13

Docta

"Pih," said my spirited grandmother Manyu Miriam, "you notice I have not bothered you ever since you sent word you were not going to witch doctors anymore." We were sitting around the fireside one evening waiting for dinner to get ready.

"Ma, they are not to be trusted. See the many times they have promised to treat me and it doesn't work? They're fraudsters."

"Not all of them, my daughter." She sounded doleful to make me feel I was mistaken.

The *docta* she had in mind this time was a young man, reputed to be very powerful owing to a cryptic visit from the world of the spirits. His fame had spread widely as someone who could cure all sorts of incurable diseases.

"Ma, do you know I could have contracted a dangerous disease from the old, rusty razors they kept using on me? They keep a single blade for months, using it on every client who comes in for treatment. That's a very risky practice. It can kill people." My argument had a smack of bookishness.

"They are changing now. The modern ones ask you to come with your blade yourself. I have one in my bag here."

I realized my point was countered, so I put forth a different argument. "You know that even the Bible is against such dark practices, Ma. Their powers are not from God." I had picked up an interest in Bible reading as I began coming of age, hoping to answer the many questions forming in my young, inquisitive mind.

"This one is different, Pih, I tell you. I wouldn't have come to you if I didn't notice that he was." She enumerated the ways in which the new *docta* was different and modern, including the fact that he never began any day's work without praying and had an open Bible before him at all times.

She had even brought a witness, my distant uncle who had been a chain smoker for many years. "Look at Johnson." Uncle Johnson let out a loud cough he had been stifling while our debate was on. His cough attacks sometimes nearly stopped his breathing. "Who would have thought he could get up from that sickbed once more? But thanks to this *docta*, he is alive and well today. Johnson, tell them if I'm not telling the truth."

My mother gave a knowing smile as Uncle Johnson got into the debate. He could barely speak with the cough as he explained how his life had been brought back from the brink because of the powerful doctor.

I had pushed my luck a little far in arguing with my grandmother. I let Uncle Johnson ramble on as Mami dished out our food. She, I trusted, would have the final say.

Mami decided we should give it a try, although we had laughed at the incongruence of the stories of healing put forward to make the case for the *doctas*.

I had promised myself never to go to witch doctors again. But I had an obstinate hope that one day I would walk again, grow up like everyone else, and take command of my fledgling dreams. It was enough to make me rethink my stance.

When we arrived for our consultation, we met a yard full of people awaiting daybreak. They had come early to take their numbers. This was a common scene at most *doctas'* places. Going to the hospital was a luxury only a few could afford. Our families' economic situations condemned us to this life. A culture of suspicion married with illiteracy made many of us easy prey for charlatans.

My turn to go into the *docta's* tent came around mid-afternoon. My mother offered her shoulder as my crutch as we rose from the waiting area, a long bamboo bench placed on the veranda. As we entered the little room, the pungent smell got stronger. It was a scent I had smelled a little too often, usually around witch doctors, and it left me nauseous.

Mami let me sit on the lone stool placed opposite the *docta*. A young man sat cross-legged on a mat and exchanged greetings with my mother. Between two lit candles, a huge open book lay before him, presumably the Bible. A range of statuettes lined up according to size on both sides of his mat completed the décor.

He counted beads in his left hand and threw cowries with the right. He now turned to me. An overgrown moustache and bloodshot eyes gave him an almost frightful appearance. My heart missed a beat.

"I hear you did not want to come here?" he growled, looking at me directly. "You think education came to separate us from the ways of our ancestors?" Manyu Miriam must have informed him I was in school.

He went on in a mocking tone, "Your grandmother says you have refused to come see me because you want to follow God's ways. Who do you think gives us the power to do what we do here? Don't you see that God is the one who directs us?" He gestured to the objects that surrounded him.

All the while, Mami stood next to me. It was unlike her to let me fight this battle on my own.

The *docta* went ahead to throw cowries several times, either to diagnose the cause of my ailment or to get directions on what to prescribe.

He picked up a piece of paper and a pen, something I had not seen any other *docta* do. It turns out he was more educated and modern than I had expected. He handed my mother a list of items to buy for my treatment. It included a live black hen, some locally produced eggs, boa fat, and a blanket. He advised Mami to rush to town and get the items she could get. She could leave the money for him to provide the rest.

As Mami stared at the piece of paper in her hand, he said, "Do not bother about the price. Her treatment will not go for more than two weeks. When I'm finished, you'll bring me many more things on your own to thank me, because you'll see her running around like nothing ever happened to her."

None of the rest of this was new.

When Mami returned with the items, the treatment, déjà vu, entailed placing the black hen on my head and shoulders over and over to cast off any spell that was on me. Then a foul-smelling bowl of concoctions was given to me. I drank some and the rest was used to bathe my whole body. After the bath, I returned for the routine cutting on my face and joints with a razor. I was used to the cutting by now, but it was the dark powder medicine that they put in the bleeding wounds that I dreaded most. They always claimed that the more pain the powder inflicted, the more effective the medicine. After the ordeal, we were sent home with more concoctions, powder, and strict instructions not to bathe for three days to let the medicine set in. We were instructed to massage boa fat into my body before going to bed every night and to come back for another round of cutting.

Two weeks passed by. Nothing happened. We followed the instructions for a few more weeks before I told my mother I wouldn't go on. Even a blind man could tell that no improvement had occurred since we started. Plus, I was sick and tired of going around stinking like a boa! I never set foot in a witch doctor's tent again.

Aunty Jane suggested I go to SAJOCAH during the summer holidays for physiotherapy to ward off the besetting weakness. This sounded more reasonable to me. Although I wanted badly to spend time with my family, I conceded to go. My sister Britha, then about 10 years old, came along to be my caregiver. After three months, not much had changed. I was given a pair of wooden crutches. Unable to lift them because of the weakness in my hands, I barely used them. At least I had my tricycle.

CHAPTER 14

Rites of Passage

In Form 5, we wrote the GCE O Levels. If we passed with at least four subjects, we would be able to continue to the final two years of high school. If not, we would have to repeat the exams until we finally got the results we needed. For some people, this took so many years that it ended their school journey. For my family, paying for me to sit the exams again would have been nearly impossible.

Results were to be released in August and announced via the national radio service of Cameroon. The announcer would painstakingly read name after name, centre after centre, school after school, throughout the country. Excited and expectant, we sat by the radio set for hours on end; even then, one could easily miss one's name amidst the noise that accompanied this exercise. When the radio came to our centre, everyone in our household put their hands to their lips to command silence. The noise level went from a rowdy marketplace crowd to a graveyard in a matter of seconds.

"Centre number 075, GBHS Bamenda, passed in 10 subjects . . . " the weary voice of the announcer rattled on.

We heard everybody's names: Anastasia and Adeline, as well as other classmates. Everybody's name but mine. Those whose names were read rejoiced hysterically while I pondered in shock.

How could I have failed the exam? What would this mean for my future? I had never failed an exam before. What could have gone wrong?

Thankfully, it turned out someone else had heard my name among the first names that were read. I had passed nine out of the ten subjects I sat for.

I was growing into womanhood, a bittersweet experience for a girl living with a progressive disability. Aunty Jane's knowledge as a nurse came in very handy when I experienced my first period and when I needed to start wearing a bra.

I struggled to accept these new changes in my body. I was beginning to internalize others' suggestions that the changes and weight gain were responsible for the rapid weakness that was caging me.

My cousins for their part seemed to be taking the changes in their stride. They began applying makeup at all times and sewing their school uniforms a little tighter to show off their emerging curves. On occasion, I caught their conversations about boys: which ones were more generous to them than others, to give in to marriage proposals or not to.

While suitors began to come to them in numbers, boys hardly looked my way. I listened to other girls narrate their experiences from the sidelines. I kept my crushes on the male folk in the deep secret chambers of my heart. I longed for a bit of the attention these girls my age were getting. I envied some of the gifts they received from boyfriends on their birthdays,

Valentine's Day, or Christmas. Some of the lack of teenage relationships may have been a result of my shyness, but it was an open secret in my culture that a girl with a disability was unfit for a relationship and marriage. I felt people saw no deeper than my pretty face on a broken body.

My cousins, however, were good "wife material". In Form 5, Anastasia's parents began pressuring her to choose one of the many suitors interested in bringing her into a matrimonial home. Her family members saw marriage as a panacea for her and the family.

She resisted. She preferred to pursue her education instead of early marriage – she was only 17. We both dreamed of growing into independent women together, capable of travelling the world and owning our own cars and houses.

The family members persisted. They used every trick in the book to persuade her to get married, warning her against waiting so long and missing out if she lost these opportunities in her prime. She finally succumbed – on the condition that she was allowed to continue to go to school.

The marriage ceremony was held shortly after the GCE results were released. It had all the trappings of an African wedding ceremony: new and expensive printed fabrics for the couple, extended family coming together to celebrate with much wining and dining. It was the first marriage ceremony I had attended and I enjoyed every moment, sharing in my cousin's glamour and joy.

As was our custom, the bride lived with Aunty Jane for a few days after the wedding ceremony before being sent off to her own home.

The morning of the send-off was very busy as everyone helped Anastasia put together her belongings to get started in her new life. She came into the bedroom to bid me goodbye. I dreaded seeing her leave. We had grown closer than sisters, sharing more than a room together all these years.

"*We go see nor?*"[1] Anastasia said to me in her usual jocular manner.

"*OK, we go see,*" I responded in Pidgin English. "When will you start your registration?" That same morning, Papa had come to start the process of registering me into high school for A Levels.

"They say I should hold on until I settle before I think about school." She shrugged. "Maybe next year I won't be together with you in GBHS." Her words confirmed my suspicion that we were not going to see each other again for a long while. It hurt to think about this.

It dawned on me then that her family did not plan to keep their promise. After all her bargaining, she might never finish her education. She was following a path that everyone expected, but it was a path that I knew would have destroyed me. Perhaps there was a blessing that came with my disability.

But with Anastasia moving away, will I even be able to continue my education? Moving in step with Anastasia since our days in primary school meant she understood my needs more than most people did. Her faithfulness as a caregiver left me wondering what would become of me now that I had to return to school in a few weeks.

Before I managed even to say "goodbye", I lost control and began to sob.

She hugged me and wiped away the tears. "I'm not going too far. We will see each other again soon." I nodded, and then she left.

---

1 "So, I'll see you later . . ."

As everyone went out to say goodbye to the new bride, I joined my father, who had been waiting in the living room.

"So, Mom, I came so that we could see into your registration. You know schools will soon resume."

"What are we going to do now that Anastasia has gone, Papa?" Both of us knew that this was the inevitable challenge to tackle.

"I have thought about that countless times. I don't seem to get an answer." My father went on to name the various possibilities he had considered, including bringing my kid sister to live with me and help. But there was no primary school close enough for her to attend.

"I think I would just stay here and write the GCE from home next year," I proposed as we considered the options.

"No way! You cannot stay at home away from school. We'll look for a solution."

"But what solution is there, Papa? I cannot live on my own and there is no one to help. This may be the only way."

"No," my father insisted. We stood together in silence for a while.

"I don't understand, Papa, why my life is so difficult." I could hardly contain the frustration that was welling up. "Just because one person leaves, my life has to crumble."

"It's not so. There will be a solution," my optimist father continued, struggling to make his words convincing.

I shook my head in anger and resignation. "Papa, I have thought about this over and over but there really is no solution. I don't know what to do."

The helplessness in my father's eyes made me even angrier. I knew how much he wanted me to go to school, how much he had sacrificed to get me here, how much he swelled with pride every time I had good results in school, and how much it meant for him that I stay in school and be successful in life.

We both sat, letting our thoughts jitter in the silence of our minds.

I bowed my head to hide the tears that started streaming down my face. Footsteps at the door indicated that the train of people that had gone to see off Anastasia was returning. My eyes caught my father's for a brief moment.

For the first time, I saw my father cry.

CHAPTER 15

Needy

Never one to let challenges deter him, my father convinced me we had to keep moving until we encountered help on the way. I returned to GBHS Bamenda, staying in the same tiny room that had been my home for the most of five years prior. Once more, he stuck around for a few days into the new school year, coming in very early to assist me to prepare for school, pushing my tricycle to and from class, and then leaving for home in the village. Taking care of me after Papa left inadvertently fell to Fongwi, Anastasia's younger sister. Thankfully she attended the same school as me, along with my other cousins, distant and close.

Poverty's ugly fangs were sinking deeper and deeper into my family's daily reality as this year went by. Ever since Papa's accident, we were becoming more dependent on the produce Mami got from subsistence farming in the village along with my other siblings. It was barely enough to feed our large family. The benevolence of some friends and family members came in from time to time, but things just seemed to get worse by the day.

My father explained that because he was unable to afford books and fees for that school year, two of my siblings had to stay out of school. I nodded in quiet acquiescence, feigning strength without, screaming within.

I was fortunate to be able to stay in school. I understood the most basic of school supplies was all my family could provide, so I jealously kept the few books I was given, reading one text over and over until I got a chance to borrow another from a classmate.

I retreated more and more into the magical world of books. Less verbose, more pensive, I buried myself in a book during the hours of break from one class to the other, or in the afternoons as I waited for someone to give me a push home.

In this way, I read all the volumes required for our English literature classes before everyone else. Ngũgĩ wa Thiong'o's *I Will Marry When I Want* did more than prepare me for the English Literature class. It reinforced my belief that life came with way too much injustice and suffering. Richard Wright's *Black Boy* took a profound toll on me. I immersed myself in the segregated world of black and white America in the early 20th century. I began to form a parallel between our life stories – Wright was enslaved by some individuals' shameless racist ideology and I was enslaved by the shackles of poverty and the inevitable weakening of a debilitating body. We both needed to be freed!

In A Levels, students narrowed their field of study to three to five subjects of their choosing. Along with English Literature, I signed up for French Literature and History. Only the English Literature classes were held in our regular classroom, which was accessible enough for me to attend. I still had to park my tricycle outside the class, crawl up a few steps, and grab the wall to get into that classroom. Since many students had signed up for History, the only place that could hold all the students was a more spacious but very inaccessible hall away from the regular classroom. French Literature was also held in an inaccessible room, but during a period when our regular classroom was unused. My plea with the teacher to transfer the classes to our own classroom fell on deaf ears. She held firmly to the room apportioned for her by school authorities. This meant that for most of the school day, I missed History and French Literature classes. I sat by myself, reading, recopying lecture notes, or watching classmates come and go as they shuttled from class to class.

Some days, after a night of many questions and tears, I stayed at home. I couldn't be bothered to go. Aunty Jane had fallen sick, so I no longer went to her house on the weekends. Fongwi helped when she was around, but she would often leave for several days. Unlike Anastasia, who had arranged for someone to help me when she couldn't be there, Fongwi didn't seem to understand that I was dependent on her to do basic tasks.

Other times, staying away from school was not so much a choice for me as a condition imposed by my circumstances. My tricycle, after a few years of use, was now old, rusty, and rickety. Its inflatable tube tires were constantly punctured, requiring frequent visits to the cobbler's shop. Someone's attempt to steal one of its hind tires from our veranda one night left the tire hanging so loose that it often gave way while I rode to school. Papa made countless trips into town to take it for repairs. While I waited for him to come from the village, I locked myself up in my little cubicle, bemoaning my unfortunate lot and reading.

One afternoon, my classmate Claire came running to my room after school. "They want to see you in school," she said, struggling to catch her breath.

"Who wants to see me?"

"The principal came to ask after you in class today. We said you've not been coming because your tricycle is broken down." She sat on the wooden chair by the window. "Someone came to school today, asking if there were people who needed wheelchairs. Their organization wants to donate some wheelchairs to needy people."

My friend could hardly contain her excitement. Claire was amongst many schoolmates who were very concerned by my frequent absence from class and went out of their way to give me a debriefing of the day's lessons after school, lend me their textbooks, bring me food, and even come around to clean my room.

If my indifference puzzled my friend, she did not let it deter her. I was at a place of deep anguish and bitterness. I was beginning to see everything through a cynical lens.

Claire continued, "Imagine! If you get a wheelchair, then you'll be able to go to all the classes, because your chair will go right inside. You won't have to leave it outside and crawl into class as is the case with the tricycle."

I nodded as she went on enumerating the benefits of having a wheelchair for me. I was slightly amused by her enthusiasm, considering it naïve trust in the tales of Cameroonians who ran charity organizations. I had heard one too many stories of their greed and deceit, taking advantage of the weak and vulnerable like me.

At the end of the day, I decided to give it a try. The lady who came to our school happened to be a nurse from a local hospital, who worked alongside others in the charity organization. She had left her contact address for me at the principal's office.

The following day, I borrowed money from a neighbour to hire a taxi to the hospital downtown to meet her. I waited for hours but couldn't see the "Good Samaritan". She finally answered with a note, asking me to come to the Bamenda Municipal Stadium on the following weekend at 9 a.m.

This promise of a wheelchair began to arouse my hope from its slumber. It was one good thing happening to me in a season of despair. I could barely wait for the announced Saturday morning to come. Without my tricycle to go to town, I was obliged to hire a taxi once again. In these dire times, it seemed a fortune. But I didn't mind – it was for a worthwhile cause. Aunty Stella, my mother's last sister, accompanied me to the stadium before leaving for her daily routine.

I had not been back to the Bamenda Municipal Stadium since the night of disappointment at Reinhard Bonnke's healing crusade years before. Memories of the rowdy crowd played in my mind over and over as we awaited the wheelchair distribution to commence.

An amphitheatre-like arena with plastic chairs was arranged to welcome many. A few more people trickled in and sat on the chairs around us, persons with various types of disabilities accompanied by family members. After about three hours of waiting, a pickup truck pulled up.

The organizers offloaded its contents: wheelchairs, crutches, and an assortment of other gifts. My heart leapt. *Finally, I'll get a new wheelchair!* They took another hour or so to unpack and conspicuously place the equipment for the cameras. The rains came before the unpacking was done. I had been seated in an exposed area of the field. The rain drenched those of us who could not move away by ourselves quickly. A flurry of speeches went on as we resettled and dried off from the rain. The downpour made it impossible to hear any of the points they read. *Who cares about your carefully crafted speeches? We came for mobility aids!* I couldn't wait to get my wheelchair and go home.

More waiting. Then a few persons were called up and offered crutches. *The wheelchair receivers must be next in line.* A few more items were handed out, and then they started packing the rest of the equipment into the back of the pickup truck.

Apparently, everyone was aware that the ceremony was at its end – everyone but me. As soon as the rains abated, people started trickling out the same way they came.

I felt like screaming. *What is going on?!* Everyone went by, indifferent to the injustice I was getting sick of. I found myself left alone once again, with nothing to do but cry. My tears caught the attention of one of the ladies doing the packing, who came over to see me.

"Sister, can I help you?" She bent towards me with concern written over her face.

I had never felt more humiliated. I could only manage to shake my head. I couldn't even wipe the tears from my face successfully with the back of my active right hand. Perplexed, the kind lady went over and called a few of the organizers of the pseudo-event, a man and a woman.

The woman spoke first, "Did they register you to receive something today?"

"Somebody came right to my school to ask me to come," I said between sobs.

She turned and whispered to the man with whom she came over, before turning to me again. "Ok, so we'll give you a pair of crutches."

My courage returned as rage. "You have no idea what I have been through just to get here," I blurted out. "For weeks I have not been able to go to school, because my tricycle is broken down. I don't have food to eat, yet I made sure I borrowed money to come here because they told me I was getting a wheelchair."

"The only thing we can offer you right now is a pair of crutches."

"Crutches?" I snorted. "What am I going to do with crutches? Look at my hands, I cannot hold anything, how can I use crutches? You have wheelchairs in the car over there! I need just one of them, please." I cried.

"Well, sorry, we're not distributing wheelchairs today." With that, they turned and walked back to the pickup truck.

CHAPTER 16

Despair

For the next few days, I sulked in my room. I wished I had never been born to see my hard life. I blamed God. I cried at night and during the day, asked questions, and threatened to end my life, all the while expecting some grand miracle to come from above. None came.

I grew even more frustrated and angry. That fellow humans disappointed me was bearable, but to be disappointed by my Creator? I couldn't take it.

It's better for me to die than to keep living.

A *Reader's Digest* story from Aunty Jane's house wouldn't leave my mind. Entitled "A Window of Hope", it told of a beautifully talented young woman about my age who battled cancer. I had cried profusely when I read that she succumbed to the killer disease.

I compared my life to hers. We were about the same age, but we had been born in different worlds. Hers was a world of abundance, where doctors diagnosed diseases and sought a cure even to the very last breath. She passed on, but her life had inspired research that was helping save the lives of other children suffering from her form of cancer. *Not exactly a life wasted.*

But mine? I doubted it would be considered "A Window of Hope", too, if I ended it right away. My life seemed obscure and useless. This thought hurt me more than anything else. We had never discovered what condition I had. *Am I the only one in the world who suffers this way?* Like Job in his travails, I wished I had died at birth or along the way like my friend Rosemary. Why hadn't God swapped my lot with that of my stillborn sibling? *Why would a good God create a beautiful body like mine and go about breaking it again?*

Or is God good at all?

Is he all-powerful?

Is there a God?

If I took my life, would anyone notice that I wasn't there? Maybe my family. Would anyone miss me? Would anyone write my story, the story of one little girl in a small, unknown part of the world, who had so many dreams that never came to pass? Would it be featured in a newspaper article, a magazine, or even a book someday?

At least the girl in "A Window of Hope" had that legacy. I dreaded oblivion. I had always wanted my life to count for something, for something significant. If God cared enough to create me, or anyone else for that matter, in his image, then it could not be in vain. That is what the Bible taught. It was what I had been taught since Sunday school.

But now, the more I thought about it, the more I concluded that my life was without purpose, without impact, an empty wind blowing without meaning.

Frustration became anger, and anger grew into ugly rebellion and bitterness towards God. I stopped reading the little New International Version Bible Papa had offered me. I also stopped making any effort to attend church service at Presbyterian Church

Ntamulung, the local church not far from our school and home, where I had been going occasionally. This was my way of shaking my little fist at God for all the hurt I was feeling, all the pain he was causing me. My warped mind made me believe I could use God for my own ends.

I lay in bed on many a night crying my eyes out. I listened to chirpings and cooing outside and played the scene of my funeral over and over in my mind.

I imagined family members crying around a plain wooden casket, rolling over and rubbing themselves in the dust. My mother and my siblings carrying their hands atop their heads as they mourned. It would be painful for a short while, but then everyone would be relieved to go about their lives unperturbed. It was a great idea.

In the dark shadows of despair, the little whisper was growing louder that life was not worth it. I chose to listen.

I picked a blunt knife to self-inflict a fatal wound that would end it all for me. But the knife was either too blunt or my emaciated hands too weak to apply the pressure needed.

I turned to a local bleaching agent that I had heard was a more effective venom. This too did not succeed.

The problem was, when I replayed the scene of my funeral I pictured Papa. He would stand stunned over my dead body, unable to cry. The thought made me cry all the more. I couldn't bear to imagine what my death would do to my father.

Looking back, the fear of breaking my father's heart kept me from trying harder to end my life, but even more, my Father God was watching over me.

We were nearing the period for the end-of-course examinations. Girls and boys clustered in groups of four or five discussing their plans for life after high school. I watched and listened from my front desk position as if I were in a totally different world. But for my friend Michelle, I would have sworn I was a pest in their midst.

Michelle Obale came to the public school after failing in her final year GCE Exams in a more prestigious confessional school. One very early morning when schools had been going for a few weeks, she found me alone in the classroom. As usual, I had come earlier to evade the traffic that ensued from the influx of students pouring into our school. She was timid, pretty, very polite, and wiser than the bunch of girls who went around seeking to be noticed. We bonded instantly as I helped her situate how far the various subjects had gone and recopied some of the notes she had missed. She chose to sit with me for most of the classes we attended together. This irritated some of the girls who wanted her in their clique.

Because she was from a rich family, she had been provided with all the textbooks prescribed on the school prospectus. This was a tremendous blessing to me and other classmates who didn't have textbooks in many subjects. Once more, I could read topics before the teacher brought them up in class.

I had custody of her books as the more studious one. Every time a book was returned, Michelle and I rummaged through the pages. After circulating among the students, they would often come back with funny little secret notes of boys and girls who wanted to go on dates with each other. Michelle and I often laughed about these. Other times the books contained practice exam questions and attempted answers that we read and corrected without the knowledge of the owners.

One day, I was going through *A History of Cameroon* by Victor Julius Ngoh, a popular but scarce text among classmates. It had just been returned by Irene. I came across a note addressed to Bernard, another classmate with whom she was known to hang around a little too often. My lips curled in a mischievous smile as I unfolded the note. As expected, it spelt out in black and white her feelings for Bernard.

What I hardly expected was her reference to me as "that crippled thing" who stood between her and friendship with Michelle Obale. *How many others in class see me as "the crippled thing" who doesn't deserve to be in their space?*

Her note deeply hurt my feelings and opened my eyes to the way some people perceived me as a girl with a disability. I questioned my place in the world.

I decided against sharing this note with Michelle and observing if she, too, would treat me differently. She still returned from every break time with a bag of Alaska and fish roll[1] for me, even when the others literally dragged her to go along with them. Unknown to her, some days this was the only food I had to look forward to.

After careful consideration, I concluded that the view of Irene and others like her wasn't representative of the whole picture. I could still count some people who loved and appreciated me the way I was. I chose to dwell on those who accepted, loved, and supported me. I resolved that my life would be a blessing to them. Irene's words began to lose their sting.

To cement my resolution, I took up red thread and stitched a reminder on the little white hankie that had dried many a tear from my eyes: "I'M NOT GONNA CRY, NOT NOW, NOT EVER."

---

1 An ice lolly and a fried roll with fish filling, a favourite snack of students.

Of course, I have cried a few times since I stitched the words, but every time I lifted the little hankie to wipe away tears, I was reminded that they didn't come about because of someone's wrong perception of me. The shock and anger of Irene's note was the beginning of the end of my desire to have others' opinions validate my existence.

CHAPTER 17

Books and the Author

Other people showed kindness and kept the flicker of hope alight in my heart. My classmate Pascaline Nahjola caught me crying in class one day with my head hidden under the desk. She saw the teardrops I was trying to hide on the dusty cement floor. Unable to get any information out of me, she insisted on following me home to the tiny room.

When she saw the empty but dirty, soot-covered pots atop our kerosene stove, she asked, "Do you have anything to eat?"

I shook my head, feeling too helpless and humiliated to speak. I couldn't bring myself to tell her I had not had anything to eat for a few days now. So intense was the hunger that I sat dazed in class, unable to follow lectures, unable to do anything but cry. This year, Aunty Jane suffered from a protracted illness, so my mother had no time to farm or to bring me food regularly.

My friend dashed out. Before I could clear my tears, she was back bearing a plastic bag full of raw food. "It's all I could find at home."

Though she lived with a distant relative and had very little herself, she made sure she brought me food whenever she could. Sometimes the only reason we lack is that we do not ask.

Pascaline also gave me a book that she thought might comfort me. *My Son Johnny* by John Edmund Haggai recounted the painful ordeal of a couple caring for their son with severe disability. He was born with terrible brain damage and had to go through life in the prison of an inadequate body.

How could a couple be grateful to God for a son who lived out all 24 years of his existence in a vegetative state, totally dependent on others for every personal need? I was not 24 yet and I still could do a few things by myself, but every fibre of my being yearned for healing. Johnny's parents had a tenacious faith amid their suffering that I hadn't heard talked about before. I thought faith in Christ was meant to make my life better, not to strengthen me to trust God through affliction. I expected healing, not acceptance.

Before I had time to recover from the shock of reading Johnny's story, another bombshell dropped. Another classmate, Jackie, stayed behind to study after school. She was moving back and forth with a small paperback book in her hand. Jackie was considered a very strict born-again Christian and not very close to me.

As she passed by my desk one more time, I finally summoned the courage to ask, "Jackie, please may I see your book?" She stopped. It had a simple cover, graced by a beautiful white lady's face, with a simple title: *Joni.* "Are you reading it now?"

"One brother in church asked me to read and return it tomorrow, but I've not had time to."

"So can I borrow, read, and give it to you tomorrow?"

"Well . . . if you're sure to finish it by tomorrow."

"I'll finish it." Judging by the volume, I could finish it in a few hours. It was lighter than the bigger books I read through in a day.

As such, I was introduced to the world of Joni Eareckson, an athletic, spirited teenager who lost her independence and dreams, along with the use of her limbs, in a diving accident at age 17. I barely blinked until the last page, finishing it before I got home that afternoon. I had read hundreds of books at this point, but never had a story so resonated with me.

I was learning for the first time about someone losing the use of all their limbs – *quadriplegia*, she called it. *How can someone possibly live like this?* I still had some use of my limbs to get around and do basic things on my own, but already I felt that it was impossible to go on with life this way.

Unable to sleep, I got up several times in the night to read portions of the story that had felt much too real for me, too similar to my own story. *Maybe in her country, it is different,* I reasoned in response to the worries cascading in my mind.

What if . . . ? I could not bring myself to utter the words. I raised my eyes towards the heavens, seeing only the familiar brown wooden ceiling of my room. *Please, God. Don't let this be my life, please!* I feared nothing more than losing all mobility, losing my independence, and becoming completely wheelchair-bound. It was the ultimate humiliating thing I could imagine.

Yet I saw myself in Joni's place: losing mobility and independence, crying "Why me?" to God when others were worse off and deserved worse, challenging God's love and wisdom in letting a tragedy befall me. Her parents, like mine, felt the pain just the same and poured themselves out in many ways to allay it. Our stories, though set thousands of miles and many years apart, seemed to bear the trappings of the same Author.

Only one difference stood out. Joni had resigned herself to the Author's will. She trusted good to come out of the gloom and despair, letting God write her story. I still stubbornly challenged the Author. I had a very long way to go.

Joni conspicuously quoted from Romans 8:28 in her book: "And we know that all things work together for good to them that love God, to them who are the called according to his purpose" (KJV). *How much good would she ever see from her condition?*

I compared my life to hers. I saw the banal tasks I could still do for myself that she couldn't: brushing my teeth, using the toilet, bathing, and feeding myself. I had taken these for granted. *How ungrateful I've been all these years, choosing to focus on the little speck of getting healed, rather than the whole beautiful spectrum of blessings God has wrought in my life!* In light of these two most recent reads, I had a lot of blessings to count, if only I would.

Joni's story birthed in me a new desire to find out the good that could come out of my pain. At night I replayed scenes of my life in slow motion to pick out lessons I could have missed. The exercise proved further that I should have been more grateful rather than accusatory towards God.

God was reaching out to me, but I was not sure how I could reach him. I had heard from several preachers that a relationship with God started with surrendering one's life and will to him, acknowledging one's sin, and crying out to Christ for salvation. Surrendering was hard for me to do. All my life, I fought God's will. This recent read began to break down prideful walls of justification and ingratitude.

Like books had a way of doing, Joni's book engulfed my world for the next few days. God's love seemed to be shining on me from an altogether new direction. With this warmth came a relentless, inescapable thudding in my mind: *What do I do now? I was wrong about God. I've been wrong all the way.*

I couldn't remain indifferent to the dent Joni's book had carved out on my soul. Looking back now, I know it was my appointment with destiny. It did not matter that it started as a casual brush with a book from a classmate; this was going to be a defining moment in my life. Like the Samaritan woman at the well in John 4, I was about to encounter the God who knew everything about me, the God who would cause springs of living water to flow from my soul.

Outwardly I seemed to be doing all right, but inside these newfound truths were like a raging current, more powerful than any before. A lifetime of personal beliefs and convictions were crumbling against their force.

For the first time in a long time, I picked up my little red Bible as I sat on the veranda after school. The only passage I could remember that dealt with God's love was John 3:16. I could recite it, but I opened and read it over and over again, letting the words sink in softly and soak my soul: "God so loved the world . . . God so loved me." Then I read Romans 8:28. The line that struck me the hardest was: "called according to his purpose".

Love and purpose summed up my quest in life. Here I knew I had found it. The rest I couldn't understand, but I figured I could entrust my life into the hands of the Almighty who gives love and purpose. My prayer was simple but sincere. I asked forgiveness from God and surrendered my will to his.

The Bible immediately took its place as the most important book for me. I read it at least twice each day before returning to my classroom books. It made more sense to me now than ever before.

Frantic students counted each day as exams approached. We created reading groups which met either in our classroom or in my room. Despite my hectic study schedule, I made it a point to never miss an episode of *Turning Point* and *The 700 Club*, two uplifting Christian television shows which aired on our national television. They clearly spoke about the gospel and shared stories of its transforming power in people's lives. I had watched them before now and recited the prayer of repentance whenever it was offered without ever fully surrendering. I had even followed and prayed along with thousands through the telecast of Billy Graham's crusades on TV, yet my heart had not been humbled to accept God's will for my life.

This time my commitment was real, so real that I copied out the postal address on the TV shows I was watching and wrote to the producers. To my utter amazement, I received a reply: a beautiful package of Bible study material which helped me take my first steps of faith.

CHAPTER 18

Visiting Aunty Jane

Aunty Jane's sickness was worsening. She had been to several hospitals, including the famed Banso Baptist Hospital. Word reached her children and me that the hospitals had sent her back to our village home for palliative care. Mami and her siblings were so busy moving around with Aunty Jane that Mami could barely farm crops for food during that year to feed the family.

It was becoming more apparent that the family could not afford to send me to university even if I succeeded in the GCE A-level exams. The thought was unbearable, but I clung to my newfound faith and hope in God. As I learned that God was my Heavenly Father who actually listened and answered me, I prayed earnestly for my future, for my family, and for Aunty Jane.

After completing my exams, I moved to Manyu Miriam's house to see Aunty Jane and wait for the results. We met Aunty Jane at the door, leaning over on a cane in her right hand. Her dress hung so loosely on her emaciated body that she looked like a scarecrow. She was nothing like the beautiful, bubbly aunt I had seen almost a year ago. She struggled to take a few steps to the outdoor latrine, leaning on her sister for support. As my eyes welled up with tears, I fought them back, reminding myself to be strong for the others who had been through the worst days of her illness.

Mami, her siblings, my grand-uncles and grand-aunties, and other distant relatives had all congregated at Manyu Miriam's house. It was a bustling atmosphere of caregivers who came and went to carry out their daily activities but stayed close enough to support one another and provide around-the-clock care for Aunty Jane. Old but still feisty Manyu Di was also present along with her sister.

That evening we all sat around the fireside, cooking and eating dinner. This was a good day, my grandmother said, compared to what Aunty Jane had been through lately. I had a hard time believing that until I heard the other stories of her struggle with HIV and AIDS. They sounded like they were pulled from the pages of a tragic novel instead of my own family life.

Later that night, I lay with my cousins on the grass mattress, listening to my snoring relatives sleeping on fertilizer bags on the dirt floor, I couldn't sleep. My mind wondered once more about the meaning of suffering. *What form of evil illness could so eat away a person's body to the point she was unrecognizable?* She had been turned away from hospitals. Everyone was acting normal, but I sensed an unspoken resignation and expectation of the worst.

"She is dying, Jane is dying in my arms!" an aunt shrieked in the middle of the night, jolting everyone awake. She was the one who slept close to Aunty Jane that night to monitor and tend to her needs.

"Everyone come and see! Jane is dying in my arms." The whole household sprang to action like a well-rehearsed army. A few people went into the bedroom where my aunt lay, others went to get what medication or concoctions were available, and the fragile older ones sat up in their sleeping places uttering prayers and incantations.

I sat on the edge of the bed, watching the action in the fireplace's dim light.

My mother, grandmother, and others desperately wailed to God for help. I added my silent pleas for God to rescue my helpless aunty. Aunty Jane's painful cries were interrupted by coughing. This painful ordeal went on for an hour or so.

"It has calmed down a little," my mother announced to the rest of the family as she emerged from the bedroom. "Everyone go to sleep; she has calmed down."

The coughing had abated and the shrieks had subdued, but I wondered whether this meant my aunt was better or otherwise. I remembered the stories of God's miraculous intervention from *Turning Point* and *The 700 Club*. Maybe if we prayed with real faith, God would listen to us and reverse a situation the hospitals had pronounced doomed. I wanted to go into the bedroom and hold both of my aunt's hands and pray for her, just like I had seen on television. I wanted to release the power of God for her healing. My conviction grew that God would do something.

"Mami, please help me to the bedroom. I want to pray for Aunty Jane."

My mother woke up some people sleeping on the floor to create space for me to move to the bedroom. "Pih wants to go in and pray for Jane."

My family members watched, but Manyu Di alone had the courage to utter their thoughts. "Aha! Jane's sickness is so terrible, God has decided to send the crippled to pray for her!" Her single loud clap expressed her awe.

Aunty Jane made it through one dreary night after the other. Some days she was well enough to recognize us, other days she sank so low we all despaired. I don't know how they did it, but my mother, her elder sister, and Manyu Miriam constituted a tenacious force that calmed us whenever Aunty Jane got into a crisis. Yet even a stranger could tell the toll her illness was taking on my maternal family. My grandmother, Manyu Miriam, was famed for single-handedly raising nine children and trekking everywhere for her palm oil trade. Amid this great trial, even her indefatigable strength was waning.

We lived knowing that death was in the very next breath. In the afternoons we all sat around the fireside, roasting corn and listening to the September rains dance on the corrugated iron sheets above our heads. The family was weary and I prayed some good news would come our way.

My GCE results were released, but with neither a radio set nor a phone connecting us to the rest of the world, we didn't hear the results for two weeks. When my Aunty Stella went to Bamenda, she brought back a copy of the local newspaper that carried GCE results.

Everyone, including my grandmothers who could neither read nor write, was eager to know my results. In my last year in high school, I had added Religion and Philosophy to my other three subjects. I secretly nurtured the dream of breaking a record: I wanted to pass in five GCE Advanced level subjects in the arts for what I believed was the first time in the entire country. I may have been losing my mobility, but I needed to prove to myself and others that I hadn't lost everything.

When I got the paper, I opened it to centre number 075. My audience of expectant family members held their breath until I looked up from the paper and smiled.

Everyone was happy, announcing to the others as if they didn't already know. I asked Mami if I could go in and tell Aunty Jane.

I sat on the edge of the mattress where my aunt lay. Very little light drifted in through the crack in the mud brick wall and the partly opened window into the bedroom. The pale figure on the bed struggled to breathe. I still had a hard time reconciling her to my aunt. Her beautiful face seemed at peace, though gaunt, tired, and wrinkled. I reached and touched her fingers – tender and more slender than I knew them. A tear began to roll down my cheek as I imagined how many times these hands had held me ever since I was a baby. Memories of the stories she told me about our trips to the hospital when I was a baby made me smile.

A bout of coughing brought her out of her peaceful slumber. She stared at me intently until she recognized me. "Mom." Her voice was barely audible.

"Mami," I whispered.[1]

"You've come to greet me today." She grabbed my fingers a little tighter. "God has been good to us, Mom. God has been good."

"Mami, I came to tell you I have passed the GCE."

"My daughter has passed the GCE. God, I thank you." She tried to raise her feeble hands in a gesture of gratitude. I was 18, but she pulled my face closer, rubbing my cheeks to dry my tears like I was still a baby.

"I always knew you would do well. I will not be here to see it, but I know God will take you places."

"Yes, Mami," I said in between sobs, "and he will keep you to see his miracle."

"When I am gone, take care of . . . " a violent cough stole her last words. The cough got more and more intense. She was about to pass out.

---

1 In my culture, we call our aunties and uncles Mami and Papa, just like our parents. Aunty Jane had been like another mother to me.

I screamed for my mother. She came rushing into the room along with the others. They hurriedly carried me out while struggling to administer medicines. A disturbing silence descended on the bedroom after a few minutes. We waited outside for the worst.

The look on Mami's face when she came out reassured us that Aunty Jane was still alive.

The following morning, I prepared to go see my father a few kilometres away in our family home. I was holding on still to a flicker of hope that some miracle would happen and I would see myself going to the University of Buea.

I left my grandmother's house early in the morning, along with my two-year-old brother Jevis, hoping to catch the first cars that came out and to avoid the heavy late afternoon showers. During the rainy season, it was extremely difficult to commute within my village. The muddy earth road was too slippery for the regular rickety old cars that plied the road. Heavy lorries transporting Irish potatoes from the village to supply nearby cities did little to help the roads.

A distant cousin with an overloaded taxi dropped us halfway. The hassle of untying my tricycle from atop the car and getting me into it so consumed us that we forgot the little bag containing our clothes.

The motor park seemed strangely devoid of any village taxis. A few people sold items here and there, chatting in our mother tongue and laughing cheerfully. I looked around for a convenient place to park my tricycle while we waited. This park seemed to be on a slope, for everywhere I turned seemed to be heading downwards. I finally chose a spot by the road underneath a tree where the protruding roots served as brakes and where my brother and I could be shielded from the sun and passing cars.

A few hours went by, but no cars passed by to carry us home, only lorries. Passers-by were concerned, including a classmate from high school in Bamenda. She was surprised to see me and said taking one of the heavy lorries was our only option. I protested vehemently. *How would I board a truck like that?*

The day progressed. Dark clouds gathered. I finally succumbed to my friend's plea to consider the lorry option. She arranged with a driver and strong boys to carry me and my tricycle into the lorry. The difficulty of getting into the high vehicle was every bit as bad as I had dreaded, but get into the juggernaut I did.

Jevis joined me in the tiny front compartment of the old lorry. Then the driver, a tall, dark man with a moustache, got in. Before long, Jevis was asleep in my lap.

The driver began taking a detour from the road I was familiar with. He read the look of concern on my face and tried to allay my fears.

"We go pass for Menka, take some potato before we dey go."[2]

By now, the drizzle had become a heavy downpour. My friend was right; the lorry defied the slippery dirt roads like no other small car could dare.

I noticed the driver's long glance at me from time to time. I imagined the disturbing stories I had heard about hot-blooded truck drivers. To keep from catching his eye, I stared down at my brother, holding on to make sure he did not fall in his sleep. I tried to pray and distract myself by picturing what was happening at my grandmother's house.

---

2 "We'll go through Menka to pick up some bags of potatoes before we proceed."

My thoughts shifted to the young man at the back of the truck, the driver's assistant in charge of loading the heavy bags of potatoes into the truck. My heart went out to him with the heavy rains pouring down on him. *Why couldn't he be brought into the lorry's cabin to be sheltered? An extra soul in this cabin might help keep the truck driver's lecherous eyes at bay.*

The lorry came to a sudden halt as we approached a slope on the road. The rain was easing too. *Why had we stopped?* I couldn't see any bags of potatoes waiting to be carried. The driver seemed amused at the look on my concerned face. Winding down his window, he screamed, *"John, bring chain."*

"Patron, you say weti?" the man in the back screamed back.

"I say make you move chain," he screamed even louder, pronouncing other insults and curses on the poor man as he pulled back his head into the vehicle. John climbed down with a bunch of chains and began to tie them around the wheels of the lorry to give the tires a better grip.

The driver turned my way. I chose not to look at him. He reached out and held my left hand. His hands were big and rough.

"I beg you no touch me, I beg." My plea seemed little more than senseless noise to him.

"So you be think say we go waka came reach wey something no happen eh?"[3] His hand began to crawl up my arm.

I closed my eyes in disgust and kept on pleading. *"I take God name beg, no harm me I beg."*

He continued, caressing my neck a little. Tears began to stream down my cheeks. His rough hands slipped under my shirt and wandered around my chest. I knew my feeble arms were no match against this burly man. There was nowhere to go in the tiny cabin, and my brother was still deep asleep on my lap.

---

3 "So, you believed we would travel to the destination without something happening?"

Unable to fight back, I prayed silently. Muscular hands kept fondling my breasts. All my life, I never felt more helpless. I sobbed, hoping John would finish whatever he was doing before the driver went any further.

The chains stopped rattling. The driver abruptly stopped touching me and pulled down my shirt as John came close.

"*You don finisham?*" the driver asked, pretending to be calm.

"Yes, patron," John responded. John was the answer to my prayer, saving me from experiencing my greatest fears with the lust-consumed truck driver.

After the initial relief, a fuming rage rose inside of me and rolled in hot tears down my cheeks. We rode on for the rest of the trip without looking at each other or uttering another word.

CHAPTER 19

Dreams Deferred

Two days later, word reached us that Aunty Jane had gone home. The inevitability of her death did not slacken the blow it had on us. It was decided that nearly everyone would travel to bury her with Mami. Jevis, my little faithful brother companion, and Elvis, who was down with malaria, stayed back with me.

The family had to halt whatever preparations were underway for the school year. It was early September, and my brother Elvis and cousin Linda were preparing to begin secondary school. Their excitement was dimmed by the very sad news, which left us all wailing for many days. A cloud of grief settled over the whole family, leaving us unable to deal with anything else. With Aunty Jane gone, so were my floundering dreams of beginning university that year.

This tested my newfound Christian faith. I claimed promises like Jeremiah 29:11 about God's irrevocable plans for my life, or Proverbs 3:5-6, which says, "Trust in the Lord with all your heart and lean not on your own understanding; in all your ways submit to him, and he will make your paths straight."

To keep my sanity, I spent the school year teaching my siblings in the village and visiting with relatives in Bamenda. Occasionally I would receive word from those of my classmates who had moved on to the university. Those who stayed behind or got married were growing their families or learning a trade. If ever I felt different and lonely, it was during this year.

With no books to read, I listened to my father's little transistor radio for most of the day to keep abreast of goings on. For news within Cameroon, we listened to the CRTV, the state radio. To know what was happening under other skies, we followed the Voice of America and the BBC, which came through on short wave. Papa, a news freak himself, would listen through the night. He would give me the radio the following day early enough for me to catch two shows, *Daybreak Africa* on VOA and *Network Africa* on the BBC. Papa had made peace with my goal of becoming a journalist rather than a lawyer. Unbeknownst to me, this fervency was fine-tuning the future broadcaster in me.

On days when the batteries were too low to power our radio, I had to wait for my father to get a new pair of batteries from the market. So, I would make up fairy tales and rhymes for Jevis and other siblings and cousins. The stories started building an audience, who demanded I repeat some of the tales on particular nights. I thought up tales that reflected my experience of being different and undeterred.

I tried to keep a brave face, but my family knew how much not going to school was affecting me. Every evening when we came together to pray, one of the first requests out of children's and parents' lips alike was that God would provide for Hilda's schooling. Papa and I had started talking about how to make school happen for me the following year, although we did not know exactly how. People came around to try and convince my parents it had all been a waste of time to educate a child with a disability.

For instance, a few months earlier, when I was still living in Bamenda and awaiting my results, I had gone to visit my parents in the village. I finally found a driver who agreed to tie my tricycle atop the car for the minimal extra fee I was able to offer.

With the tricycle and other cargo around the body of the car, it looked like a machine from another world. On these arduous roads, the drivers used their dexterity to fit in as much cargo as possible, both human and otherwise.

We had to make a detour to drop off some people at a funeral in another village. The car, once stopped, would not start again. Off the driver went to the next town to get the needed car part. I waited in the taxi until the sun began to go down and people left the funeral. Finally, I spotted a step-grandmother, Mama Sabina.

Desperate not to spend the night in the taxi, I mustered what vocal strength I could and screamed out, "MAMA!"

"Pih, wh- what are you doing here?" Mama Sabina cupped my face in her hands and used her thumbs to wipe the tears from my cheeks. Others joined her around the car, chiming in that they had seen me sitting in the car since morning.

"Do you know this lady?" one person asked.

"I have been passing and seeing her seated in this car and wondering why she wouldn't get out," another joined in.

"Don't you know Pih, my crippled daughter?" My grandma turned to the crowd as she explained, "She is a smart and excellent student." She stepped back a few steps and pointed to the roof of the car. "Don't you see? That is her *bascou* on top of the car."

Some men unloaded my tricycle. Its cushion had fallen off on the way, but I sat on its bare bars without complaining. They pushed me up a steep hill to the main road.

A very old Land Rover soon came along with space for everyone going in that direction. Seated on my tricycle, four men lifted me and four men inside the car received me. My grandmother and the rest of the passengers crammed in.

An older man moved closer to us. With his eyes fixed on me, he leaned forward slightly to speak to my grandmother. "Sapi," he said, using her maiden name, an indication he was older than her, "I don't see why you people go through so much trouble with this child, making her go to school and all that. Such children are good for one thing: to be given to someone like me to produce beautiful children."

I shuddered at the thought. Many families were happy to let older men in the village unburden them of their disabled daughters. Few of my peers would choose a wife who was so dependent on their care, so I had little hope of relying on a husband to provide for me. I would have to provide for my future if I were to survive.

As the critics came, I silently vowed to prove them wrong. I felt like Joseph, who had been thrown into a dark pit. I need faith like his to keep going, to believe that my path would brighten up for good and that a day of rejoicing would come. I prayed for Joseph's grace and wisdom to take trials like him, to be able to say: "You intended to harm me, but God intended it for good to accomplish what is now being done, the saving of many lives" (Genesis 50:20).

One day I sat in the yard, drawing in the dust with a stick to teach Jevis how to count. A car stopped and we both looked up. Cars seldom passed on the road at this time of the day, much less stopped. It was our cousin Baba, who asked for our father with a sense of urgency.

Before I could provide an answer, he muttered, "You need to come to Bamenda. Some people want to see you."

"OK, which people?" I was curious.

"Just tell Pa when he comes back so he can bring you to town." With that, my cousin dashed back to get into the waiting car.

I had no clue who needed to see me in Bamenda, but I already felt this was another answer to our prayers.

When my father returned from the farm that evening, before he sat or shook the dust from his body, I blurted out, "Papa, we have to go to Bamenda."

"Anything the matter?"

"Baba passed by here today and said someone wants to see us there."

"Baba?" A raised eyebrow indicated he needed clarification.

I went on to explain which Baba it was, amongst my numerous cousins named after our grandfather or *Baba*.

My father smiled, nodded, and asked for a cup of water.

"So, shall we leave tomorrow?"

"We'll see how things go."

I waited a few minutes before pleading again. "But Pa, you know if we don't act fast, it could be like other chances we have missed." My mind was running through the other times when people, impressed by my results in A Levels, had made appointments and promises to help me continue school, none of which ever amounted to anything.

"You're right, but you know we have to get your tricycle fixed before we think about any travels."

In my excitement, I had forgotten about the breakdown of my tricycle, which rendered movement within the village impossible, let alone travelling the distance to Bamenda. By this time, any attempt on my part to stand upright resulted in a dangerous fall. This was another phase I was adapting to. I resorted to lower objects to make any movement. The only means of movement I had presently was a little bamboo stool that helped me crawl around the compound.

Papa was right; there was no going to Bamenda without a mobility aid. Later that evening, we conferred. Papa would go alone to find out why I was needed in Bamenda and also use the opportunity to fix my tricycle.

After a couple of days, my father returned from the city with excellent news. Ladies from my alma mater had instituted a small prize for the female student who emerged best overall in the previous year's A Levels. The award had been instituted only that year, and it covered the repairs for my tricycle. The hand of providence was at work in an apparently hopeless situation!

After the GBHS Ladies learned that I was not able to enrol in university immediately after A Levels, they committed themselves to doing everything in their power to get me into university the following academic year.

Spurred on and organized by the Ladies, in the few months that followed, my father and I joined the Ladies in a fundraising campaign. The message was loud and clear: a poor, disabled girl was unable to continue school despite graduating top of her high school class.

To see a girl with a disability who had completed high school was very rare in my hometown. To see one who was the best student was strange, but for her to aspire to go further in education was beyond comprehension for many people in Cameroon at this time. This mindset partly contributed to the timid response to the campaign to get my education funded. It was going to need more than a single girl doing well in school to reverse the predominant narrative that children with disability were a curse.

The Ladies, however, were not giving up, my father was not giving up, and neither was I. Much more, God was not giving up on me. We knocked on many doors and even managed to secure interviews on local radio and appearances on national television.

My poor father was thrust into the spotlight with me. We were often juxtaposed as a vulnerable, needy pair of father and daughter, the former on crutches, the latter on a tricycle. My concerns about it being demeaning for my father to be portrayed in this light were eclipsed by the closeness that the experience brought to us once more. Like in my younger days, Papa and I were sharing a seat on the journey, moving together, eating together, and sometimes sharing the same precarious sleeping situation.

My always optimistic father used this time to drive home his message that I stick to my dream, work hard, and not let any difficulty deter me. He would say again and again, "You see, this is the fruit of hard work. If you didn't make it with good results, these ladies would not have come to help you."

For my part, I knew how happy good results made my father. I was secretly vowing to make him even happier if given another chance to continue school.

CHAPTER 20

The University of Buea

The promise of a scholarship from the ladies of my alma mater gave me the confidence to begin preparing for university the following year, although many details were still unclear. I couldn't wait for October and this new chapter in my life. It would be a chapter in which I would live in a different town from my family for the first time in my life. A chapter in which I would no longer wear uniforms but my very own dresses to school – or was it lectures?

After losing my bag of dresses on the trip from seeing Aunty Jane, I had very few wardrobe options. I skipped going to church on some Sundays because I hated wearing the same clothes every week. I had heard that students who came to the university fresh from high school were often ridiculed due to their sense of fashion – or lack of one. This was an opportunity to prove my mettle. I had always loved "designing" dresses, although I had no money to get a new wardrobe. I reached out to cousins who were seamstresses to execute the designs I drew for my clothes. When Tewah, my kid sister, travelled for the summer holidays, I made sure she returned with used clothes that I could take along.

Tewah was all ready to come along and be my assistant in Buea, the university town. However, my mother thought that Tewah's brashness and short temper would make her an unsuitable companion. She insisted that Elvis, with his sobriety and patience, would be a better fit. Despite our pleas, my mother's astute wisdom won out.

The ladies from my alma mater promised to secure a room for me in the university hostel, but they weren't successful.

When the time came to move to Buea, my father went ahead a few weeks before to do the preliminaries. First, he had to secure admission for my little brother Elvis. He also had to find a room for us to rent. Many of the rooms in the far-off city of Buea were built with wood. Rumour had it the boards were so loosely knit that passers-by could easily peep and see the occupants inside. I told my father, whatever he did, not to pick a room built with wood.

When he returned with news that he had picked a wooden room, I swore in my fury that I'd rather not go to school than live in that accommodation.

It turned out he had picked the wooden room not only because it was cheap but also because it was accessible enough for me and within walking distance of the university campus. Once again, I had let my selfish ego and short-sightedness blind me to the care and wisdom of my loving father. I resolved that in the future I would trust that my father always had my best interest at heart.

Six years separated Elvis and me, but we were in for an adventure together. Secondary schools reopened earlier than the university, so I joined him a month into his school year. I found him suffering from a bout of malaria, a malady that would often come back to plague us over the years in Buea.

Papa stayed around for a few more days to watch Elvis recuperate, during which time, crutch in hand, he was taking me to class and back. That my father and I constituted a curious pair was no news to me. I had become used to turning heads and raising eyebrows in my hometown, but here in a new town, I felt uneasy. The only reason I was able to keep facing these stares was that Papa was by my side.

Papa's prior visit to Buea had laid the groundwork for me in more ways than one. In his excitement about having his daughter in university, he went around showing my results slip to one-too-many people, bragging about how I had been the best student in my high school. Never one to divulge my life in public, I felt embarrassed every time a teacher or other university staff member stopped me on campus to congratulate me. I soon got used to being recognized and questioned by total strangers. For most people, this was their first time seeing a young girl in a tricycle at a university.

I soon began enjoying my time in Buea. Elvis and I established a daily routine. We got up early enough for him to finish chores and take me to school before making it to his classes up the hill at the Bilingual Grammar School Molyko. Between classes, kind-hearted classmates helped get my tricycle up and down flights of steps, to and from various lecture halls.

After school, Elvis joined me again on campus. On days when we had a full day of lectures, he waited outside my class until we finished. He would playfully shove the tricycle and then hop on, perching with the agility of a monkey on the tricycle's little back carriage. Others began to envy us as we sped past them, zipping our way through campus.

Many couldn't help but marvel at a little boy sacrificing for the sake of his sister! It also paid off that Papa had made friends (for himself and me) on the campus. Occasionally when someone stopped me to ask after my father, they slipped me a discreet gift to buy some basic supplies.

I wish I could say the skies in Buea were always so bright. Some days, we considered packing up and going back home. Some days, no one showed up to help between classes and I had to wait in one spot for unbearable hours while missing lectures. As the older sister, I felt responsible to care for my brother. Many times when Elvis was down with malaria, I felt so helpless all I could do was cry and pray. Of course, there were also moments when we ran out of every scrap of food and money we had, and we felt like we were going to starve to death.

When sickness or hunger lingered on, they became a platform to test my faith like never before. Elvis and I read the Bible and prayed together. I couldn't forget how the providential hand of God had led me thus far. God was teaching my brother and me to depend on him and demonstrating his unfailing love.

During the final exams in my second year, we got ready to go to school. Elvis kept going outside to gauge the intensity of the showers. It had been raining all night and the rains showed no signs of abating. The clock was ticking. Through the window, we could see people rushing to campus with their umbrellas. Elvis could not push the tricycle and hold an umbrella at the same time, so we put on some protective clothing and dashed out. My stationery was wrapped in a waterproof plastic bag, tucked between my wet back and the wheelchair seat.

I got to the exam hall, drenched to the core. Elvis helped me out of my dripping sweater. Exam papers were passed around. I waited for my mind to settle down.

I watched heads bent over wooden desks, frantically scribbling exam responses. Whenever I could not keep up with others' writing pace because of the weakness in my hands, I tried to stay focused and process my thoughts so my answers would be concise. A few moments into the exam, I picked up the pen to write.

My fingers were numb from the cold, making my fingers even stiffer than usual. I gave it another few minutes and tried to write. My fingers would not cooperate. After many attempts, I could only write down a few words at a time.

Panic mounted and tears of frustration welled up as I stared failure in the face. Not much time was left. I resolved to not hand in a blank answer sheet. With sheer grit, I scratched down answers however I could. I am not sure how far I went before the invigilator's call came to hand in our responses. I could barely read my writing. I prayed as I handed over my script that the Lord would not let my efforts be in vain.

I remember the exact moment I got word that the results of our exams had been posted on the notice board. I was fellowshipping with other believers at a Campus Crusade meeting. I immediately thought of the course I did not write well. I designated two friends who were rushing to check their results to bring me back news of this dreaded course.

I had a C. This would have been a matter of concern under other circumstances, but at that moment it seemed like the best grade I had ever been awarded. I cried as I joined others celebrating success in their courses. When we sang "Great is Thy Faithfulness" at the end of the night, I was happy to "Join with all nature in manifold witness / To thy great faithfulness, mercy, and love."

Another evening after a very long day of classes, I watched students scamper out of the hall. No one had offered to help take me home; they were all striving to get home before it got too late. I waited for Elvis, counting the empty wooden benches before me.

I remembered how, years before this, waiting would have angered and triggered comparisons in my mind. *God must surely be transforming my heart,* I thought with a smile. *How else could I stay in a lonely place after an exhausting day like today without nursing resentment and wading in bitter waters?*

Footsteps interrupted my thoughts. I gave a guarded look at the door, expecting cheeky Elvis to step out in an attempt to scare me. It wasn't Elvis. As the footsteps grew louder and more numerous, I understood another class was leaving the isolated U Block of classrooms. The footsteps faded. *They've left me. I'm all alone in the building. I should have asked them for help!*

Where could Elvis be? Buea was a land of strange happenings. I tried not to think of what could have happened to him. I bowed my head on the front rest of my tricycle and asked the Lord to help me. My tiredness got the best of me, and I dozed off.

A gentle tap on my shoulder awoke me.

"You don wait sotey tire?" asked Elvis.[1]

"I tell you, I be dey give up," I replied with a grateful smile.[2]

Halfway home, as we manoeuvred over a stony path, he asked me to guess what we were going to eat for dinner. Only then did it dawn on me that it was another one of the periods when we had run out of food and money. I sensed mischief in Elvis's voice and decided to play along.

"The food from the village has arrived," I guessed. We had written numerous letters to our parents asking for food and money.

"No sign from the village."

"Is there food at all?"

"Something special!"

"Hmm, and you won't tell me?"

"You'll discover at home." Knowing my brother and his knack for suspense, I decided to let the matter rest until we got home.

---

1 "You waited until you were tired out?"
2 "I'm telling you, I was about to give up."

As I stepped out of the tricycle, Elvis served me a plate of rice and tomato stew! It had never tasted so delicious.

It turned out that earlier that evening he was on his way to get me from class when he met a woman carrying a baby by the roadside. She had alighted from a taxi with a load of supplies. In his typical softheartedness, Elvis offered to help her carry them. The woman rewarded his kindness with two 100-franc coins. With these, Elvis had bought ingredients. While I waited in class, he was busy cooking so I would come home to a surprise warm meal. I could never be more grateful for a loving brother!

To this day, we still recount the story of the unknown woman and the two coins. They saved us from hunger, but more than that, they taught us a lesson about God's miraculous power to provide. On days when difficulty seemed to ridicule any notion of a bright future, Jesus's words rang in my ears:

> Therefore I tell you, do not worry about your life, what you will eat or drink; or about your body, what you will wear. Is not life more than food and the body more than clothes? Look at the birds of the air; they do not sow or reap or store away in barns, and yet your heavenly Father feeds them. Are you not much more valuable than they? Can any one of you by worrying add a single hour to your life? (Matthew 6:25-27).

CHAPTER 21

Faith

As I saw God's presence and guidance in my life, I sought ways of feeding the spiritual hunger and thirst burning inside. My disability seemed to make even the path to spiritual growth less accessible.

Whenever I could venture to the nearby Presbyterian Church in Molyko, Buea, I did. However, I felt like a pariah. I tried to ignore the curious glances of many a church member. My tricycle barely fit into the crowded room, standing out like a sore thumb in the overpopulated congregation. Sometimes I had to follow the service while sitting outside in the sun. The noise made it hard to follow the sermon. After a handful of Sundays in this awkward position, I decided that going to that church was futile. I began seeking spiritual fulfilment in different places.

One Wednesday afternoon, a couple of friends invited me to Bible study at the Full Gospel church they attended. It was a much smaller and sparser building than I was accustomed to. When we arrived, I sat in the back to avoid drawing too much attention to myself. I noticed furtive glances my way as the brief singing and clapping went on.

A man took the stage and prayed. He explained that he was not well enough to teach and so he handed over to another teacher. As he sat through the study, sweat broke out on his face and his shivers increased, both symptoms we had all come to self-diagnose as malaria. My heart went out to him.

At the end of the Bible study, he struggled to stand up from the bench. He asked the teacher to delay the closing prayer. When he started making his way toward me, I knew what to expect.

Without asking, he laid both hands on my head and started praying in tongues. He invited others to join him and before I knew it, the entire group encircled me. Those who could reach out and touch me did, all speaking in different kinds of tongues. This was not very familiar to me, so many people praying with loud voices in strange languages. *What was even stranger,* I thought as my friends wheeled me home, *was the irony of someone shivering with malaria praying for my healing.*

My cousin Dean believed fervently that I was going to be healed – if not by my faith, by his. Dean and I were age-mates who shared a lot of childhood memories and quite some rivalry. We had both become born again as we moved to the university. Our conversion caused a stir in the family, who feared we had been lured into mystical groups that often preyed on naïve university freshmen. Dean leaned more towards the Pentecostal side of the faith. He knew where I stood concerning the search for miracles and he condemned my stance as a lack of faith. He had met many a charismatic preacher and sometimes impersonated those he watched on stage and on TV.

One time, I returned from school break to find out Dean had written to the American televangelist Ernest Angley and acquired a healing cloth and some pamphlets. He arranged a special session in my room during which he was to administer my healing. I played along with Dean, who truly believed this was the moment. His loud prayers in my room with porous wooden walls failed to grab the much-anticipated healing. Rather, my neighbours and landlord threatened to throw me out if it ever happened again.

Another day, I went along with Dean to a Cameroon Youth for Jesus and Academic Campus Fellowship event. He had advertised it to me as the climax of a week of enriching Bible studies he was attending.

It was an animated evening with beautiful singing and teaching that went on long into the night. When it came time to pray as the night rounded off, there was mayhem. I feared for the people who were falling over on benches and onto the concrete floor as the movement leaders laid hands on them. I prayed secretly that no one would spot me in the back.

A young lady ran hysterically up to me. She held both my hands, muttering words I could not understand as tears streamed down her cheeks. She claimed she had had a vision of me walking. A crowd gathered.

I was shaken, fearing what would happen next. I was pulled out of my tricycle. I pleaded for them to stop. The ensuing chaos drowned me out. They dragged me on the dusty floor, all the while praying and chanting for me to "rise and dance".

It seemed like a very long time before the frantic praying died down. My failure to "rise and dance" was rebuked as a lack of faith. I was returned to my chair. I was left dust-covered and humiliated with a bruised, aching body. I resolved to depend on God more and stop seeking miracles so I would never be made an object of such ridicule again.

What fulfilment I had previously sought from healing, I now sought from answers. *If God would just give me an inkling of why I'm sick, I would be satisfied. What sort of disease is this that depletes my muscles so? Why has my path been designed to be so thorny and tough? If only I knew why, I would have peace.*

Up until now, no one had succeeded in giving me a diagnosis. I set out to discover what the doctors thought about my condition. After my O Levels, I had sneaked into the office in SAJOCAH where the medical records were kept while the administrator was out for lunch. I pulled my file from the drawer and stealthily opened it, hoping to get to the bottom of my medical history. I came to the page inscribed 1984, the first year I was brought there. My heart leapt. It contained my name and other information. The part that said "Diagnosis" was blank. I was disappointed, but my quest was not over.

Another time, I learned that a group of doctors and specialists were coming from America to consult in my hometown, Bamenda. I reasoned they would have better exposure and knowledge of an obscure condition like mine. I contacted a distant cousin to bring me there very early so I wouldn't miss a chance to see the doctor.

After waiting a whole day, I was ushered into the tiny, makeshift consultation room. My heart raced as I answered the doctor's questions. He took a closer look at my hands and feet, then settled back in the chair and started writing. Unable to wait to read it later, I asked him to explain the diagnosis. He paused from his writing, straightened up and looked me straight in the eye. "I'm not sure what condition you have. Unfortunately, you shouldn't expect to live long enough to graduate from university."

I left the room with hopes dashed. I had long nursed the hope of meeting a doctor from a developed country, thinking that person would explain the weakening forces that were at work in my body. It was hard to accept that even here, there were no answers. All evening, I struggled to process the thought of not living long enough to graduate from university. Before falling asleep that night, I resolved to trust God rather than humans with my life or death. *Whatever the doctor says, God has the final say.*

I still longed to grow in my knowledge of God's Word. I read the Bible with voracity and enrolled in a correspondence course. I thought I found a precious treasure trove when I read about the man born blind: "'Neither this man nor his parents sinned,' said Jesus, 'but this happened so that the works of God might be displayed in him'" (John 9:3). These words of Jesus did much to remove the guilt I had built by listening to other teachers.

As I continued interacting with others who wanted to see me healed, the reminders were so frequent I found myself wondering if the decision to stop seeking miracles was a wise one. I wanted some confirmation from God's word that my stance was not due to a lack of faith. One night, I read 2 Corinthians 4:16-18:

> Therefore we do not lose heart. Though outwardly we are wasting away, yet inwardly we are being renewed day by day. For our light and momentary troubles are achieving for us an eternal glory that far outweighs them all. So we fix our eyes not on what is seen, but on what is unseen, since what is seen is temporary, but what is unseen is eternal.

This verse seemed to directly address and reassure my doubting mind. I finally began to understand that suffering had a purpose.

So strong was my yearning for Scripture that I invited in anyone who came in the guise of dispensing God's Word to help me grow. A group of Bible students stopped by my room weekly, but I soon found out they were Jehovah's Witnesses. Our reasoning together could not hold because our conclusions about the essentials of Christianity were diametrically opposed. Despite their encouragement to continue "research" to fuel the pointless debates, I chose to discontinue our meetings. My cynicism about the numerous spiritual groups on campus was cemented now.

By the time I returned for the second year of university, I was well prepared to avert the invitations that came my way from Christian groups and live out my faith alone. It took some convincing from a dear friend and classmate to try one more group.

Delphine Fanfon was straining to push my tricycle home from a Sociology class one afternoon as she had done many times before. Between breaths, she reminded me of her previous invitation to come for a Campus Crusade for Christ meeting. I had tacitly rejected her previous invitations, but this time, I accepted out of sheer guilt; she had shown such great patience and kindness towards me.

I sat on the sidelines the following Wednesday night in the large living room where the Campus Crusade meeting was held. I could barely join the others in earnest fellowship and prayer, holding my breath to see when they would start to pray for my healing.

When this didn't happen on the first night, I was relieved and chose to come back, still highly cautious. It didn't take me long to realize there was a difference in this new gathering. The focus was not on getting me out of my tricycle but on growing my knowledge of Christ and his grace.

The Campus Crusade family stepped in to provide spiritual nourishment and warm fellowship when I couldn't find a local church that accepted me. Here, I found a family that loved me unconditionally. As love is wont to do, it lightened the burden of the challenges Elvis and I faced. He joined me after a few months too. Here, I was taught that God answers when we ask, seek, and knock. Here, I first learned to pray publicly, lead Bible study, find confidence in my singing voice, and share the love of Christ with others.

I spent more time in the Campus Crusade ministry house than anywhere else because I couldn't drink enough from this new fountain. Thanks to a supply from the leader, Efi Walters, I began replacing my reading of sensual secular books with books on God's character and his grace. J. I. Packer's *Knowing God*, C. S. Lewis's *Mere Christianity*, and Jerry Bridges's *The Pursuit of Holiness* laid a bedrock for the Christian way and satisfied my hunger for reading.

Teachings about grace gripped my attention more than anything else. The more I learned about God's grace, the more I realized how much it was woven into my story. I saw God's grace in saving a sinful rebellious and arrogant heart like mine, in keeping me alive against all odds and the doctors' predictions, in surrounding me with family and people who cared so much they wouldn't let go. Where others had congratulated me for being intelligent and beautiful, I now realized even this was because of grace. I had come through a lot of sad days, some of which caused me to despair of life. Where I thought I had developed resilience, I now saw grace.

This also impacted my view of how life would play out going forward. I was 20 years old. All efforts to stop the progressive weakness in my body had proved fruitless. Questions about marriage, childbearing, employment, and dependence haunted me. Even these fears were getting addressed in the little five-letter word: *grace*. I learned *grace* is a person and his name is Jesus. Grace was with me at every moment and would be with me always!

Coping with my disability became harder in my second year of university when my faithful tricycle began showing serious strains of wear and tear. The usual breakdowns were aggravated so much that I could barely use it. I had to stay home more often and for longer periods while waiting and hoping for a solution.

When the front wheel came off completely, I stayed home for a month, which worried my lecturers and classmates. They started looking for ways of raising money to get a wheelchair for me.

A suggestion was made to do a short film that would show the world the hardships I was struggling to overcome. My journalism classmates took the project to heart, but in this era before the internet and social media, it did not have much of an impact. The Campus Crusade ministry leader sacrificed to buy a new wheel for my tricycle. This did not really solve the problem. I was almost losing hope.

Then news came around that Cameroon's first lady, Chantal Biya, had donated new wheelchairs for students with disabilities in universities around the country. My hope was rekindled – until I learned it was going to be another few months before the wheelchairs were distributed to needy students. My studies would suffer fatally if I had to wait for another few months.

As time went by, a list came out of students who had been shortlisted to get wheelchairs. My name was not featured on it. All the students on the list had disabilities, none as severe as mine. They went about their activities on campus with a limp, but only a couple of them even used canes. I wondered what they had done to be more deserving of a wheelchair than me who was stuck at home for lack of one. I wrote a complaint to the school administration and waited. I did not hear back from them.

I decided the only way was to take the bull by the horns. I would meet the vice chancellor (VC) of our university in person and present my problem. Our VC had the reputation of being a very stern woman. Some claimed she was more difficult to access than most of our obtuse and arcane politicians. Hope is bold.

With Elvis, we worked out how to get to campus with the sloppy old tricycle. On the way, I fell off and scraped my arms and knees. When sensitive onlookers offered to help clean my wounds, I turned them down. My tears and blood would speak for me.

We arrived in the morning and Elvis parked me beside her deluxe Toyota in the parking spot with her name on it. People stopped by with words of encouragement, while others made cutting remarks.

I waited as the sun got hotter. The director of social services came by and tried to talk me into returning home. I was determined to meet with the head of the university or spend the night in the lot. Evening approached. I noticed many of those working in the administrative block leaving.

Someone opened the rear door of her car and dropped a little suitcase in. *If this is her driver, she must be coming out soon.* I braced myself.

The VC emerged through the main door, elegant in her trademark silver curled hair and simple flowing African-print dress. As she carefully descended the porch steps, I tried hard to think of what to say. All I could call up was tears. It was like a reel of my entire existence until now ran before my eyes and all I could see was pain. I wiped my eyes before she got close enough to see.

"Good afternoon, Ma." First greeting her was the culturally respectable thing to do.

"Good afternoon." Her response was matter-of-fact. Someone must have informed her there was a poor, disabled girl beside her car. Perhaps she had seen my tricycle through the tinted windows of her car whenever we moved over to let her drive by on the campus street. I introduced myself and explained how I had written to her office on many occasions to seek assistance. My on-campus hostel room was denied. My tuition exemption was denied. So was this latest request about the donated wheelchairs.

"I badly need a wheelchair, Ma. I have been home for over one month now because of this broken tricycle. I even fell today from the tricycle as I tried to come and see you." I cried as I spoke, stretching out my arms and lifting my skirt to show the dried-out blood.

She nodded and promised to give instant instructions for me to receive a wheelchair. I thanked her as she got into the car.

As the VC's car drove off, deep humiliation and frustration swept over me again. I hated that I always had to stoop so low to beg for things that everyone else seemed to have easily. The tears rolled out freely for a little longer, but before Elvis came to take me home, I felt confident enough to announce we were not going to be hobbling around with the old tricycle for much longer.

I waited, but I still did not get the wheelchair. Finally, I heard rumours that some people in her administration felt

I was disqualified from receiving such a gift because I came from another province of the country and was not a "daughter of the soil". Petty politicking and the ugly head of tribalism were surfacing everywhere.

Second-semester exams were fast approaching, and I was not sure I would sit them. It took the courage of Dr Enoh T, the head of our journalism department, to confront the clansmen. On the brink of giving up, I was called up one afternoon to come for the wheelchair distribution. The campus terrain was unfriendly, yet it made a world of difference to finally be able to access more places for the rest of my university days.

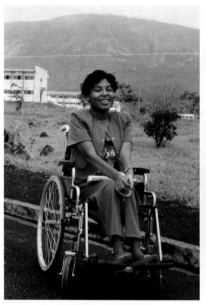

University of Buea,
first days in a wheelchair

Elvis and me,
graduation day

Congratulations from the Vice Chancellor

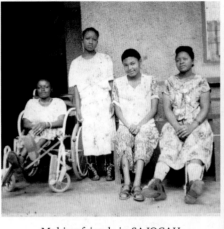

Making friends in SAJOCAH
(L-R: Elizabeth, Odette, me, Prudentia)

With Britha
in SAJOCAH

1999: With Papa in Buchi,
Pinyin on my tricycle

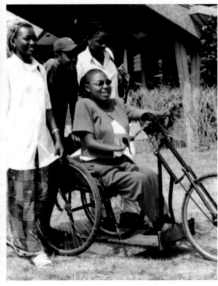

Between lectures at University
of Buea with friends
(L-R: Ali, Elvis, and Quinta)

CHAPTER 22

Graduation and Beyond

Graduation morning. *I made it!* I wore a fern green dress that Tewah had brought the previous day from Bamenda. Shoes and makeup were provided by my cousin Destine, who had joined us at the University of Buea too. I adorned myself in my graduation robes with satisfaction that early November morning. Elvis looked almost perfect in a black waistcoat, black trousers, and a white long-sleeved shirt as he wheeled me to campus for what was going to be one of the last times.

My parents and other relatives had come to celebrate this milestone for my family. Their presence gave a festive air to the whole event, coupled with the congratulatory messages and cards that were coming my way.

On the way to the graduation grounds, many people who hadn't known I was among those graduating recognized the robes. Elvis and I were treated like celebrities as people stopped to offer us gifts while others simply wanted pictures of and with us. They congratulated Elvis for deserving the recognition as much as I did. Every tearful, rain-drenched, or hunger-infested period seemed to pale in the pomp of this day. So often my needs and struggles had been overlooked by the administration. As people celebrated our hard work, we both felt vindicated.

I had not fully grasped the significance of my presence at the university until this euphoric moment.

To crown the glorious day, I was singled out to receive a prize. The Vice Chancellor in charge of Academics read my name among the honour students. A round of applause followed. Then he stressed that it was the student who used a wheelchair. It became a standing ovation.

The cheering continued as Elvis pushed my wheelchair down the steps of the open amphitheatre where the ceremony was held. We struggled up the flight of steps on the makeshift podium to receive congratulatory handshakes from the Minister of Higher Education and the Vice Chancellor. I glimpsed my father in the audience; no one in that crowd could have been prouder. He recalls to this day the standing ovation and the handshake I received from the Minister of Higher Education as if it all happened yesterday.

"What will you do on your last day in Buea?" Elvis had asked me this question several times as we had dreamed of returning to our hometown, leaving behind the challenges we were facing in Buea. Answers varied depending on the circumstance of the question.

However, when the time came to leave, more questions arose than we could answer. *Where will I live when I return to Bamenda? Where will Elvis continue going to school?*

My bachelor's degree was in Journalism and Mass Communication. New radio stations were coming up in Bamenda. It was still daunting for me to apply to work in them due to the inaccessible infrastructure of most.

For a time, I stayed in Buea and volunteered with Campus Crusade for Christ. I received financial support from an American missionary friend I had met at a conference organized by Campus Crusade. I had noticed her kindness right away. We fondly called her "Mama Carrie" for her love for us. Her monthly gift of 50 dollars was a lifeline which ensured survival for my brother and me.

Eventually, it came time to move on. It was not an easy decision to move to Bamenda alone, while Elvis stayed on in Buea in school.

I soon moved again from Bamenda to the village to be with my parents. I found great difficulty settling in. The years spent at university had rendered me weaker and more dependent. Elvis was far away, and Tewah had moved away and started her own family in Bamenda.

Britha, my much younger sister, stepped up to fill the shoes of the absent siblings as my main assistant and caregiver. She rose early and made sure I was prepared for the day before heading for school. My parents made sure to stop home during the day from their farm work or other preoccupations to help me. Each time they had to leave home for a few days, they would figure out who would stay with Hilda. The constant care made me feel like a helpless baby all over instead of a grown woman who had just graduated from university.

It didn't help that some classmates of mine had picked up jobs with radio stations already. My father and I heard them on air on our little transistor: "The news read by . . ." Whenever the name was familiar, I would excitedly announce to Papa and the entire household, "That's my classmate," with a tinge of jealousy and concern in my voice. I had performed better in school than most of them.

The more I spent time in the village, the more old, ugly fangs of comparison, bitterness, and pride bared once more. The years spent in the university had seemed like a light bulb of hope lit up to guide my path into a bright future, but here I was in the bleakness of village life again. *Was God turning off the light?*

I felt caged once again in my impaired body, a feeling which brought out the worst in me like nothing else. Having lost financial support, fellowship with Christian friends and family, and reading material, I felt like I was losing my mind. I was experiencing a new form of isolation, where I was in the presence of people I knew – my own family – and yet felt like a stranger.

I clung to whatever old book I could redeem from the wooden box that housed old schoolbooks from me, my siblings, and Papa's old bookshelf. I listened to the radio until the battery ran down to a screeching sound. Still, loneliness engulfed my soul.

Often, I daydreamed that I lived in an alternate world, a world in which I had a healthy body and could be anything I wanted to be. I had developed this alter ego years before, a version of myself who couldn't be held down by anyone or anything. The Superwoman version of Hilda helped me dream myself through some tough moments. This time it was different, maybe because going to university seemed like the ultimate sacrifice from which I now expected dividends. Each time I tried to get back into this world of possibilities, something seemed to happen to keep me in the real world.

My mother sensed my loneliness and sought ways to assuage it. She cancelled visits to places that would take her far away from home and even reduced her farm work. Her efforts increased my frustration, making me feel like a guilty baby when I should have been the one helping my parents now.

Finally, it became unbearable.

I recalled how after graduation, people who had loved hearing my voice on the campus radio station had recommended where I should go next. One suggestion was to take a trip to Yaoundé, Cameroon's capital city and administrative headquarters, to apply for a job with the state broadcaster, the CRTV. Another idea was to apply for work with the soon-to-be-created Baptist Radio in Bamenda. I settled for the latter, reasoning that the Baptist Radio would provide a nurturing environment to grow my faith and serve the Lord.

I suggested to my parents I would brave the odds, go back to Bamenda, and try getting a job. My parents were concerned, knowing that I couldn't cope on my own. The new station, we discovered, was only taking unpaid volunteers. In my naïveté, I never considered how I was going to cope with finances. We agreed to call it a "step of faith". I needed it to avoid a nervous breakdown.

The inevitable question arose: where and with whom to live? We pondered this together by the fireside for many evenings. Eventually, we concluded that in my state of dependence, the only house with modern self-contained facilities that could accommodate me was my late Aunty Jane's. Ever since her passing, the relationship had broken down between my family and her husband. I didn't exactly expect a warm welcome as I undertook the trip.

CHAPTER 23

Unwelcome

I arrived at Aunty Jane's house in Bamenda to an icy cold reception on a very wet afternoon. In this house, I had known unforgettably happy moments, shared special growing-up milestones with my cousins, cried tears, and laughed hilariously. With each person, I shared a special bond and a particular story of adventure. My uncle was a father figure whose kindness over the years had introduced me to a new world. His vast collection of movies, music, and books had kept me company on many lonely days and taught me the ways of life. But Aunty Jane's death seemed to have driven an invisible wedge between us and sucked up whatever conviviality existed among us.

My uncle, not one to feign affection when he felt none, was seated on a couch with his feet resting on the table.

"Papa, good afternoon." I rolled my wheelchair closer as I greeted him. He responded without taking his eyes off his game of solitaire.

He didn't budge as my cousins dragged me and my drenched bags into the house. Even my cousins barely seemed excited. One would have thought I was a complete stranger coming to visit.

Thankfully, the new woman of the house stepped out to greet me. She knew about me already from stories my cousins shared with her. She wasted no time in making sure I was dried from the wetness and offered a plate of *garri* and okra to eat.

I later explained to my uncle that I had come to Bamenda to follow up on my application with the Baptist Radio or see if I could get a job elsewhere. I hoped it would help thaw his iciness. If the idea of me working was laughable to him, he never made it known to me; I continued to receive the same indifference that welcomed me on day one.

The next morning, I took a taxi to the Baptist Centre, where the radio house was located. In moments like these where I had no assistance, I chose to ignore any warning signal my body was sending me and trust entirely in the goodness of humanity and the faithfulness of God.

A jovial taxi driver helped me in and out of the taxi and onto my wheelchair. He listened patiently as I explained how he had to fold and pack the wheelchair in the boot of his car and how to open it up. When we arrived, the cab driver turned down my offer for the taxi fare. I was grateful I could make it for another day.

Each day, I knew my commute was going to be tough. I prayed for God to send the right people my way. I needed assistance, but I had experienced what it felt like to be home alone, and it felt better to try going out. This was the "step of faith" I had told my parents I was taking.

A few days went by. I was making new friends and acquaintances, who offered hope and respite as they made the burden a little more bearable. I felt a sense of belonging in this new sphere where professionalism and faith mingled, though I still had to go back to the house where a sense of rejection was almost palpable.

The first day we met, Ntunyu Mangoh offered to take me home in my wheelchair from the Baptist Centre. Young, handsome, and fresh from high school, he was considering where next to venture on the educational journey. His quest brought him to the burgeoning radio project, which could be a foundation for a future career. I was hesitant to accept his offer. No one but Elvis had taken me such a long distance on such rough terrain. But I didn't have enough taxi fare for the rest of the days, so his persistence won and bonded us in a friendship that continues to date.

Ntunyu worked under the supervision of Kah Abel, an amiable and ebullient sound engineer. He was a household name; we grew up listening to him on programmes produced by the Cameroon Baptist Convention on our local radio station in Bamenda. Mr Kah, as he was known to us, recorded my first voice trial on the radio. From then on, he unceasingly encouraged me to keep going with my dream. He offered to come home and do recordings if there were days I couldn't make it to the radio house. Fearing the hostility at home, I declined his offer, but I was encouraged all the same.

Then there was Vivian Maku: pretty, petite, and gutsy. She handled radio programmes in French. Our first encounter was timid, but as days went by, our lives began to be enmeshed in more ways than one.

One morning, Vivian overheard me explaining to Peter Ngong, the pastor who headed the radio venture, why I could not keep on living in Bamenda. My uncle was running low on patience, and he had made it clear to me that I was no longer welcome in the house. His kindness was blighted by the belief that living with a disability meant I was good for nothing and probably stuck in his house for years on end. I tried to ignore his frequent biting comments, hoping to prove him wrong. Finally, he forbade his children from helping me around and sent word for my parents to come get me. I knew then it was time to go, probably back to my parents in the village.

I was secretly hoping for some miracle from the church family. When Pastor Peter expressed his sympathy and his inability to help, I was distraught.

Vivian found me crying in the tiny studio later. It seemed no hope was in sight. I was feeling caged again, unable to stand on my own to follow a dream. She dried my tears and reassured me that something could be done to keep me coming to the radio.

"The main problem is not even coming here but getting a place to stay," I explained to her between sobs. Holding my hand, Vivian encouraged me to hang in for a few more days.

Vivian concluded that I had to be in the city to keep my dreams aflame, and she set out to make sure this was made a reality. For the next few days, she knocked on every door she could, hoping that my time working as a volunteer with the radio would elicit compassion from the convention leaders. She pleaded with the leadership of the church, imploring them to consider my desire to serve without pay even with the challenge of being in a wheelchair. She made no headway.

Vivian and I had one last desperate move. The Director General of the Cameroon Radio Television was a notably religious and magnanimous man. Some people told me if he could set eyes on me, qualified as a journalist and in a wheelchair, he would offer me a job. He was in Yaoundé. We hatched a plan to travel there together.

The day before the journey, Vivian and I came over to my uncle's house. We pored through pages upon pages in the phonebook looking for a number we could use to contact the office of the Director General for an appointment or even to confirm he would be in the office. Our countless calls yielded little fruit.

When my uncle found Vivian with me late that evening, still hoping to make the right contact, he sent her out of his house in a most humiliating way. He was enforcing a new rule that didn't let visitors stay after 8 p.m. Vivian took the incident kindly, picking up her handbag, bidding good night, and leaving. For my part, I felt so embarrassed I knew I had to move before anything worse happened.

The next day, we left Bamenda late in the afternoon for the seven-hour bus ride to Yaoundé. We planned to arrive in the night, try to meet with the benefactor the following day, and head back to Bamenda overnight.

We didn't know where we would spend the first night in Yaoundé. We couldn't afford a hotel and I had no relatives in Yaoundé. Vivian, who had gone to university there, knew lots of people but their homes were either too far out in the suburbs or not accessible for my wheelchair. We spent a few hours at the bus park after we arrived trying to find lodging for the night. Yaoundé was a noisier and more vibrant city than Buea or Bamenda, the other towns I had lived in. Its buildings were taller and closely knit. Its streets were always busy, even late into the night. Its drivers were as impatient as the town was hectic.

After many futile tries, I remembered a distant relative my father had told me about who lived in Yaoundé. His insistence that I take "Uncle" Michael's number with me seemed prescient. We called and Uncle Michael not only took us to his home that night, but he also took us around the town the following day. We tried and failed to get into the premises of the national broadcasting house to meet with the director and later to see the Minister of Social Affairs.

The trip proved a futile and naïve move. We had neither considered the hassle of getting to a "big man" in Cameroon, nor the political climate at the time, which was right after elections. Vivian vowed to continue clamouring for help. I, on the other hand, felt totally beaten.

I returned from Yaoundé to my uncle's house and prepared to head home to the village. I was giving up on any hopes of staying in Bamenda, of getting employment, of following my dreams, of a future.

I had always chosen to believe against the odds I could live a successful and independent life, even with a disability. During moments when this dream seemed to be waning, my father was standing close by to fan it to flames. All my life, he had drummed into me the belief that if I worked hard enough at school and got a good education, I could become anything I wanted in life. In the face of my present difficulties, I remembered the people who said that educating a disabled girl was pointless. Maybe they had a point. Maybe Papa and I were wrong all along.

CHAPTER 24

The Courage to Wait

"I remain confident of this: I will see the goodness of the Lord in the land of the living. Wait for the Lord; be strong and take heart and wait for the Lord" (Psalm 27:13-14).

These words of the psalmist I had written, along with other Bible verses, and pasted on the wooden walls of my room during my university days in Buea. They are the very words I wrote out on a card for a fellow brother going through a rough time as I left Buea. This confidence in the Lord's goodness was the buoy I clung to as I felt myself sinking into the depths of despair.

Wait for the Lord, I would struggle to tell myself when I couldn't cry anymore, couldn't sleep from the anguish of a soul wearied by protracted trials. I spent my last few days at my uncle's house in the bedroom I shared with my female cousins, trying to keep out of his way. He expected me to be gone, so he treated me as non-existent.

I longed for Aunty Jane's comforting presence. There were times when everyone was gone, the house so eerily quiet, that when I stared at her room across the hallway, I expected her to burst out with gusto as she had in life. Of course, it never happened. I cried all the more.

I would analyse my life and conclude God was bent on pulling down every pillar on which I leaned. As I lay in bed one afternoon, after another bout of crying, my conversation with God went something like this:

Lord, I really do not get it. I have waited on you.

Silence.

I love you, Lord, I do. I want to do your will, but this burden is much too heavy. I am crumbling under it. I can't go on.

Silence.

I don't doubt your love for me. But how can you love me and break me so? Not just for a season – my whole life I have known nothing but brokenness and pain.

Silence.

Just a word from you, Lord. One word to keep me going. Otherwise, this is it. I cannot keep going like this. I cannot.

Silence.

This conversation – or rather monologue – with God was not leading anywhere. I had no doubt God was listening, but why he would not answer, I couldn't tell.

I drifted into sleep. It was the kind of sleep that does not completely numb the senses. Then I heard a voice: "Will you trust me?"

So still and so small, yet it shook me out of my reverie. I looked around to make sure I was still alone in the room. The same haunting silence filled the house. I was not sure if the voice I heard came from me or someone else, but I took it as God's voice.

I want to trust you, Lord. But it's so hard, I'm not sure I can do it. Then I remembered a verse on grace pasted on my Buea wall: "My grace is sufficient for you, for my power is made perfect in weakness" (2 Corinthians 12:9a). Immediately,

I prayed for grace to get over this hurdle. It was enough to get me through!

For a few more days, I held on in Bamenda to meet with Mama Carrie who was coming to town. Over the years, I had often run to Mama Carrie for help and encouragement. She would call the mobile phones of my uncle and of people around me to counsel me, pray for me, and find out about my needs. Often, she had sent someone coming to Bamenda with a surprise parcel for me. Her packages always met a pressing need. There were days when I was shunned by almost everyone around, and someone would come running with the phone to announce Mama Carrie on the line. I look back and it amazes me how much gentle words, even those spoken from a distance, through a mobile device, can soothe a troubled soul.

While I waited to move to the village, I decided to visit Aunty Francisca, who still owned a provision shop at the Bamenda Main Market. She never failed to provide soap, body milk, and other personal items whenever I came around. I figured I could get some supplies from her before retiring to the village.

She gave me so many provisions for my journey that Louis, my cousin and personal assistant for the day, could not carry them and push my wheelchair at the same time. I held on to the plastic bag on my lap, while Louis wheeled me back to the house along on the tarmac of the Commercial Avenue Bamenda.

Earlier, on our way to the market, two pastors had invited me for healing prayers in their church the following Sunday. We were still laughing at how often I had been the subject of invitations recently when someone stopped us.

The first thing I noticed was his towering stature. So tall was he that he had to stoop to address Louis and me. "Hello, good afternoon."

I could tell from his accent he was not from around Bamenda. Probably from the French-speaking part of Cameroon. "Good afternoon, Sir," I replied.

"You look very beautiful and happy." I was taken aback by his bluntness. "I am Claude, Bambe Amba Claude. I am a pastor." He extended his hand. As I struggled to untangle my hand from the plastic bag on my lap to shake his, I introduced myself and my companion. He gave us a couple of gospel tracts and explained that he had just come to Bamenda to start a ministry. He lived with his wife and children in a nearby village, and he would love to meet us again. "Is it OK if I come to the house?"

"Of course, it's OK," I answered brashly, partly to dismiss him and partly to rush home before the dark clouds let the rain slip through their loose grip.

"Where is the house?" He smiled as if his persistence amused him.

Louis described the house and its nearest landmark, the Baptist Church Musang, next door. With this, we started to move on.

He was not done. "At what time can I come to visit?"

"You are welcome at any time." My answer was meant to close the conversation.

"OK, I will come."

Louis and I made sure we were a fair distance from our new acquaintance before commenting on the encounter. So many pastors had stopped us in one day! We concluded that, just like the ones we had met before, this last pastor was not going to show up.

It took another hour to get home; I checked my email at a cybercafé one last time before leaving for the village. We were afraid my uncle would get home before us. He would be angry if he knew Louis had helped me. But a car honked just as we got into the house. Louis and I exchanged a knowing look, thinking we had struck the lucky chord and made it home just in time.

It turned out it was someone else. "Three men in a red car are asking for you," my younger cousins said. I wheeled hurriedly outside. I had to prevent them from coming inside. My uncle had thrown out people who came to visit me at home before.

One of the three men was Pastor Claude. He introduced me to the other two co-labourers with him on the new mission field in Bamenda.

"You are very welcome," I stuttered, trying to sound nice while mustering up the courage to tell them they couldn't come into the house. I whispered to Pastor Claude I had to talk to him and explained my predicament. He amiably shared with the others, though I still felt guilty about being an unkind host.

Not one to hang up his boots easily, Pastor Claude asked if I could give them a few moments out of the house to talk about Jesus. We settled on a bar not far from the house. Over a malt drink, I shared with the group how I had become a Christian a few years prior.

Over the next few days, I shared with Pastor Claude that I was on the verge of being homeless or moving out of Bamenda for lack of a place to live and a paying job. To keep me from giving up my dreams of employment and an independent life, he suggested I join his family in Awing village, not far from Bamenda, until he found a place to live in Bamenda. In my discouragement, I had resolved to discontinue my service at the Baptist Radio. Pastor Claude assured me of his availability to get me to and from work each day.

It sounded too good to be true. I had wondered if God was still with me. I had felt left out and let down by the body of Christ, which I felt was indifferent to the sufferings of weak members like me. Once again, God was proving he could take care of me and my needs in his way and in his time. For the next year or so, I got to rest from many of the struggles I had encountered, thanks to the "casual" but divinely choreographed meeting with Pastor Claude.

CHAPTER 25

Pillars

Tough times were not very far away still. There were moments when Pastor Claude travelled out of town and I had to improvise how to get to work; other moments when my feeble body reminded me I needed more help than I could get. I was learning that facing tough moments alone always proved more difficult than facing them with others. In the course of the year, Britha moved to live with us and assist me while attending the same public school as Pastor Claude's children.

In the meantime, we were looking for a paying job. We decided to make another trip to Yaoundé to meet a benevolent government official who could offer me employment. Pastor Claude drove Britha and me. Before we got to Yaoundé, Mama Carrie had arranged for lodging. It felt like a vacation for my sister and me, but it still ended in disappointment. Despite my pastor's personal connections, we were unable to get so much as an audience with the "big man"; in fact, we were shooed away like a group of beggars.

Shortly after our return, Pastor Claude dropped a bombshell – he had been asked to move to Yaoundé to continue his work. For over one year now, his family had offered the safety and reliability I had not had since leaving the university. Their departure threw me from my carefree life back into a whirlpool of uncertainty.

Familiar questions of "Where . . .?" and "How . . .?" began to resurface. Britha and I frantically searched for a smaller, more affordable apartment. Pastor Claude had left us two months' rent, but the money soon ran out. It was hard enough to return to a place of homelessness, even harder to make it to the radio station daily.

We had no choice but to live from place to place, perching with friends for short periods, all the while hoping the hand of providence would reach out again to help. My friend Vivian was still on the move trying to get help for me. For a time, she took us in to live with her and the family of her uncle while we searched still. No headway.

I ached to watch my sister struggle along with me and be helpless to provide for her, to watch my other siblings and parents, who had given up so much for me to get here, wallow in want and still be the ones to provide for me.

I reminisced about the good times with great nostalgia, angry at the unfairness of it all. I questioned the wisdom of the God who bears my life in his everlasting arms. I even questioned the very essence of my existence. *What's the point of fighting to hold on to dreams when God has chosen to knit the tapestry of my life with the darkest yarn?*

But a bright spot appeared. Mama Carrie offered to pay my rent for four months. Vivian offered to share an apartment with us, answering the question of how we were going to sustain rent payments when Mama Carrie's gift ran its course.

Elvis, who had joined us again after finishing his O Levels, Britha, and I moved into the apartment we had found in the neighbourhood of Nkwen in Bamenda. What a joy to finally settle under a roof we could call our own! All we had was a bed, a few clothes, and the kitchen utensils that had survived our days in Buea. Britha set up the bed for the both of us girls in one room, while Elvis settled for a tiny Dunlop mattress on the floor in the storeroom off of the kitchen. The second bedroom was reserved for Vivian, who would move in with us later.

We were so elated that on the first night, we put together our meagre coins to buy a fizzy drink from the nearby grocery store. This end to our days of wandering about in homelessness was well worth celebrating!

My cell phone rang, another gift from Mama Carrie. She called to ask how we were settling in. It was hard to put into words our joy at having a home after seemingly interminable months of waiting and searching. I was learning anew how scarcity and lack can maximize satisfaction. My siblings and I could barely recall a time in recent years when we had cause to rejoice so.

Mama Carrie also asked what one item we needed most for our home. A few days later, another package was delivered. It was a brand-new gas stove with two burners brought by someone who "happened" to be working with her, and yes, he had been sent by Mama Carrie to give us a stove "so we could begin to use our new kitchen".

On a visit to Bamenda, Mama Carrie invited me for lunch alongside some of her co-workers in the field of Bible translation. We had a great time in fellowship and reminiscing. Mama Carrie encouraged us from 1 John 3:1-3 to "purify ourselves" because of the hope of the return of Christ.

Then she broke the news that, having served 26 years in Cameroon, she was leaving soon for America. No one else looked shocked. They kept exchanging pleasantries over *fufu* and vegetables. I ate along, but my mind raced ahead to weeks and months without Mama Carrie on the other end of the phone to patiently listen and pray with me. I would no longer have someone sending surprise parcels to meet a great need. *Things will go back to the old days of lack and hopelessness.* When I got home, I cried.

There is great comfort in walking through dark and rough roads when you know someone is walking with you. Through the many difficult seasons of my journey, I have had people walking with me and for the most part, my courage to keep moving came from their presence and constant encouragement.

However, the longer someone walked alongside me, the more dependent I became on them. I quickly went from leaning on persons for support as a crutch to keep moving to fully putting my weight and trust in them like an indispensable pillar. My father, Achu, Anastasia, Elvis, Aunty Jane, Pastor Claude, and others had filled this void for me.

It was one of the reasons that separation from them was always such a hard blow to bear. Despite my growing faith, whenever someone I was depending on was taken away, I felt cheated like a little bird thrown out of the warmth of its mother's nest. The fear of one day living through the pain of separation was so crippling it made me wary of getting into deep relationships.

How easily our focus shifts from the God who provides to the vessel he uses to meet our needs! Dependence on humans, particularly those who come to our aid, means less dependence on the Lord, who has a way of bringing our attention back to where it should be, to himself.

The departure of Mama Carrie did create a void. Constant bouts of malaria and the inability to hire a taxi meant that I could barely make it to the radio. Elvis picked up a menial job at a bus agency in town that helped occasionally pay our bills and buy food, but this meant he had to stay away from school and study after work in the night to prepare for his A Levels.

Vivian moved in after a few months to complete the household. Her presence brought some more comfort and security. She had not waned in her push to get church officials to offer me a paying job. She met with officials of the church's health department on my behalf and returned with good news. I was going to be signing a contract to be the voice of the health department on the radio! I would produce and present content that celebrated the department's groundbreaking work.

We rejoiced at the prospect of having a paying job after a very, very long wait. Our new evening pastime became breaking down the purported budget of about 50,000 francs that would come with this new job. My first monthly salary, which would be close to 100 dollars, seemed so big. I was ecstatic that I was finally going to lift the heavy burden of taking care of me from the shoulders of my siblings and my parents. The longer I wallowed in unemployment, the more guilt I felt for burdening my family from birth to this time in my 20s. My prayer was to prove to them that their sacrifice was well worth it, and this job was going to be my first proof.

A few days later, I heard someone else on the radio presenting the very programme I was going to be doing. When Vivian came home, she confirmed the loss of the job I had never had.

I was devastated. What's more, I felt betrayed by what I reckoned was a typical instance of nepotism within the church setting. Vivian was furious, threatening to confront the authorities with a piece of her mind. The responsibility of restraining her fell to me.

My faith was shaken along with that of my friend and siblings. I barely pulled on in the days that followed, putting up a brave face in the presence of people and breaking down when I was on my own. I poured out my heart full of frustration to God. My life still seemed a dark cloak of hopelessness and disappointment.

Attending church regularly was not possible for me, but I made it a point to keep studying the Bible. Starting a Bible study for young girls around the neighbourhood helped keep me in step with God's word. I struggled to rise above the ashes of my disappointment to encourage those around me, but knowing they were looking up to me gave me the incentive I needed to keep moving. Christ remained the solid rock that kept me standing.

One morning during this particularly tough period, I made it to the radio station to find a strange woman waiting for me with a basketful of food. She explained how after listening to me on the radio she had renewed hope of living again. She had come to thank me. Our tearful meeting gave us both the assurance that our feeble efforts were noticed by Almighty God and others. We left with a renewed hope to face more uncertain days ahead. Like Job of old, I was resigning myself to a life of suffering, trusting in the God who gives and takes away. I now know that God sends various people into our lives for various seasons and reasons. When the season is done, we ought to let go. Oh, how much I still have to learn in this area.

CHAPTER 26

Microphone Queen

In March of 2006, I saw on TV that the state broadcasting corporation, the Cameroon Radio Television (CRTV), was recruiting 20 qualified English-speaking journalists. I applied.

Like all job offers in Cameroon, hundreds of people showed up when few were needed, the symptom of high unemployment among young people. I travelled with Britha to take the exams on the premises of the CRTV in Yaoundé. A Christian friend, Elizabeth Manjoh, hosted us as we navigated the noise and traffic of the capital city for days, taking written and oral exams in different locations. When it was over, we were glad to say goodbye to the mayhem and return to the familiarity of Bamenda.

The results were announced on national radio and TV a few days later. After the prime time 3 p.m. news, someone called me. They had heard my name among the new recruits!

This opened a floodgate of congratulatory visits, gifts, and messages. They came from all directions, from known and unknown quarters, from close and long-lost friends. I realized that I had been mistaken to think I had been treading alone. More people were aware of my struggles than I knew. I was indeed surrounded by a great cloud of witnesses.

The new recruits were summoned to Yaoundé immediately to be trained in the workings and policies of the broadcasting house. Even here in a place where I was relatively new, the word spread fast that a person with a disability had been recruited. In a society where disability in its various forms was maligned and very little was expected from anyone living with a disability, this sudden propulsion into the spotlight shocked our national conscience.

Perhaps no one summed it up more aptly than Philip Bawe, the renowned CRTV journalist. He met us along the corridor a few days into the new job as Britha wheeled me into the newsroom: "Hilda, I have been looking for you ever since I learned you were recruited. I just wanted to shake your hand and say thank you for not giving up." He grabbed my flimsy right hand in a handshake. "This must be the work of the Almighty God!"

I couldn't agree more. *Could it be God was letting my trials act as a backdrop so that his glory would be even more conspicuous? Did my suffering constitute the root and stems on which the flowers would later bloom?* In the months that followed, I came to realize how God can bring a weak and stubborn vessel from virtual oblivion to centre stage.

I was posted to work with the national station, the service that broadcast to all 10 regions of Cameroon. On the first day of work, Britha and I arrived more than an hour early to survey the place and get to the newsroom without raising much dust. The taxi driver was patient but curiously watched Britha lift me from the cab seat into the wheelchair.

We rolled the wheelchair to the foot of the building. I knew there were steps to get into the building, but I had underestimated how many. They rose before us like an implacable mountain. For a moment I doubted if my choice to stay and work in Yaoundé was well thought through. Britha was more optimistic.

Each day, my sister gave it all she had to pull me up and down far-flung staircases as we made our way to the newsroom on the second floor. I learned there was an elevator in the building, but when I came it was broken. Ironically, after it was eventually fixed, the elevator never stopped on the newsroom floor where I did most of my work. I hadn't realized when I accepted the position how inaccessible the then-40-year-old building was going to be for a wheelchair user. Britha's determination, more than mine, kept us going during these early days.

My recruitment as a broadcaster with a disability made news in ways I never expected. Waves of reporters from newspapers contacted me to share my story. My face beamed from magazine covers. Government ministers mentioned it in interviews as if it was a victory for the entire country. I felt like a highly valued treasure that had just been discovered and put up for exhibition.

The warmth of the spotlight was soothing for a time, but it could easily become harsh and awkward. One morning in the newsroom, we were sitting around the table listening to the editor-in-chief dish out scoops for reporters to follow for the day. A loud male voice called out in the hallway. I realized he was calling my name. Everyone paused and looked my way as if expecting an explanation. I froze.

He asked repeatedly in French, *"Où est Hilda Bih?"*[1] The man barged into the room, looking rather scruffy. He clutched some sort of portfolio in one hand. I was easy to spot in my wheelchair. He moved closer to me, moving his index finger in the air either to warn or stress something. I was not sure what to expect, but I suspected he must be tipsy. I steeled myself as everyone looked on in shock.

---

1 "Where is Hilda Bih?" While Pih is my name in my mother tongue, Bih is a variation more common in Bamenda, where my official documents were made.

"J'ai beaucoup entendu parler de vous. C'est toi que je devais épouser!"[2] He repeated the sentence a few times, then turned and went out the same way he came in.

You could hear a pin drop. Then the news conference picked up again as if the little incident had only happened in my imagination. The embarrassment of the moment fizzled into the busy workday. I never found out who the man was, but I was sure glad he never came back.

I started off at CRTV as a news anchor, a role I loved and filled perfectly. Unfortunately, it was impossible to make the quick trips from the newsroom to the studio in the wheelchair in time due to the winding inaccessible nature of the media house.

I was then called to anchor *Luncheon Date*, a more sedentary two-hour flagship daily show that relayed news from Cameroon's 10 regions. Here I was given the breadth to bring my originality to the table. For the first time, I understood that my voice counted, and I could make it relevant to thousands of people in one instant. I dug into my years of listening and following other broadcasters on the BBC, VOA, and others. I embraced the opportunity, pouring my all into it. I vowed to do so well that no one would ever regret hiring a girl with a disability.

I soon began to receive positive reviews. As time went on, people started calling me "The Voice" and "Microphone Queen". As much as the praise made me uncomfortable, it was a poignant reminder of how far the Lord had brought me, so I did not take it for granted.

Parents wrote in, called, or visited in person to let me know I was a role model to them and their children living with

---

2 "I've heard much talk about you. It's you I must marry!"

disabilities. This seemed very much like God's visible answer to my earlier question, "Why me?"

One of the shows I was asked to appear on was a radio show entitled *Role Models*, which was aired throughout Cameroon and around the region. When we recorded the casual conversation with the presenter, I responded to questions about my life with unbridled honesty. I was learning that my story could bring hope and purpose to the listeners. I was excited to finally be able to tell the world how Jesus had poured out grace on me, taking me from despair to shining hope.

Role Models aired on the radio on a Friday night. Since I did not follow the show, I didn't understand why my phone was inundated with calls the following day. When I got to work the following Monday, I was greeted by a small group of people who just wanted to know if I was the Hilda Bih they had been hearing on the radio. My "yes" was all the response they needed as the group dissolved. It turns out they had listened to the interview and come to confirm if the story I told about being in a wheelchair was real!

Even as people saw me as a role model, I still needed peers and support. My siblings Britha and Elvis were still my main caregivers. Juggling their own schedules and mine was no easy feat. They continued to make huge sacrifices. Elvis dropped out of school from the university in another part of the country and moved to Yaoundé to help.

I reunited with Pastor Claude, who helped my siblings and me find a house to rent. I joined his church and met Sara Tanner, who was a missionary living with Pastor Claude's family. I served as Sarah's translator when she taught a women's Bible study in Pastor Claude's church. She suffered from heart disease, so we resonated with each other's stories of seeing God sustain us despite life-threatening diseases and numerous doctors' prognoses. We established a bond that blossomed as we studied God's Word together and shared our tears in times of weakness.

Around this time, I also met a new friend undergoing treatment at the National Rehabilitation Centre in Yaoundé. She introduced me to another woman at the Centre, Evelyn Afombom. Evelyn had been born with a severe disability, but you could tell from first glance that Evelyn did not let her impaired body define her. Her puffy hairstyle and flawless make-up instantly announced her confident personality. Her spunky attitude belied an unbelievably disheartening story of rejection.

She shared with me how she came to Yaoundé after suffering abuse and abandonment in her native Northwest Region. Her teenage mother had birthed her and left her with the grandmother in the village. Her grandmother refused to live with her because she believed the baby to be an omen from the spirit world. She warned all the family members to stay away from the evil baby and asked for her to be killed.

A kind relative took Evelyn home. Unfortunately, while Evelyn was in her teens, her adoptive mother passed away. With no place else to go, she was brought back to the grandmother who never wanted her in the first place. Her grandmother's attitude towards her got worse by the day. Evelyn started a petty business, raising capital from gifts kind-hearted people gave her. Her grandmother finally threw her out of the house. Evelyn paid for a cab to the city of Bamenda, where a Good Samaritan rescued her from the streets and helped her get to the rehab centre in Yaoundé.

I found Evelyn's story heartrending but relevant to a society that was trying still to sweep the uncomfortable reality of disability under the rug. I pitched her story to our broadcasting house. Thankfully, the director of TV production was moved by it and pledged to come along with me personally to produce a mini-documentary.

The TV cameras and production crew kindled a fire in Evelyn's soul. She told her story with unmatched poise, speaking fluently in English, French, and Pidgin English. I was taken aback as I interviewed her because I knew she had never gotten to go to school.

Without a wheelchair, Evelyn pulled her severely disabled body around using a small plank stool. She eagerly demonstrated how she cooked, cleaned, ironed, and applied make-up – all using her maimed feet. When the recording aired on national television, many people saw for the first time what life was like for a person with a severe disability. Some people were moved to help Evelyn with funds to begin living a more independent life.

CHAPTER 27

New Horizons

Even as I raised awareness about disability across the nation, making changes within the media house proved challenging. As an African proverb goes, "After climbing a great hill, one only finds that there are many more hills to climb." I had made it my mission to make the media house more accessible to persons with disabilities, submitting pleas and notes to hierarchy. But after six years of working there, not much had been done to improve accessibility at work.

My hands had continued to weaken, making it harder to do the little things like writing and eating by myself. My siblings were growing and drifting away into new roles in their own lives. I began to sense how life would be challenging, if not impossible, in the fast-paced capital of Cameroon without the much-needed assistance of my siblings. I began to consider moving back to Bamenda, where I could rely on my parents and other family members.

In Cameroon, young people dreamed of making it in the big city. The only people moving back to rural areas were elderly people looking for a peaceful and cheap place to retire. So, when I requested to be transferred to work in the regional radio station in dusty Bamenda, I received significant pushback.

People told me, "You're at the peak of your fame. Your career is at the point everyone dreams of when they join this media house. How can you leave all of this behind?"

They didn't realize how exhausting it was for me to survive in an environment that wasn't built for me. Without the support structures I needed – physically and socially – staying was no longer feasible.

I had faith that God still had better things in store, but my colleagues' reactions made me doubt. I remembered how I had wasted away during my discouraging gap year back home. *Will my disability limit my horizons yet again? Is it time to resign myself to the fact that there are certain things my disability will prevent me from experiencing?*

Back in Bamenda, I settled into work at the regional radio station. In 2012, I interviewed the Cameroon Peace Corps Director, Jacqueline Sesonga, for the 50th-anniversary celebrations of the organization. She invited me to another event welcoming new Peace Corps volunteers into Cameroon. Drawn by her compassionate and amiable disposition, I accepted. For some reason, she was impressed with my work and was curious to know if I had visited the United States before.

Me? The United States? Of course, ever since I read of distant lands, I had dreamed of seeing other parts of the world. But I never got my hopes up because travelling around Cameroon was already a very daunting task for me. How much more exacting would wheelchair travelling by air be? While I was inwardly cynical, I knew she was only being kind, so I responded simply, "No, Ma'am."

A short while after my interview with Jacqueline Sesonga, I received a phone call from the United States Embassy informing me of various programmes I could be eligible for. My hopes were rising as I began to entertain the idea of flying. I spoke with a few friends with aeroplane experience, and they assured me that it was worth a try.

Not long after, my friend, the artist and activist Issa Nyaphagha, sent an email encouraging me to apply for a fellowship initiated by US president Barack Obama. The exchange programme was christened The Young African Leaders Initiative, then renamed the Mandela Washington Fellowship, in honour of Africa's revered statesman Nelson Rolihlahla Mandela.

Obama wanted to invest in the youth of Africa to awaken the continent's potential. Twelve young Cameroonians considered trailblazers would be selected to join others from almost every country in Africa. They would spend 14 weeks in America networking, learning how the American system functioned, and picking up new skills that would help bolster their work when they returned home.

I applied by the final hour of the deadline for the Young African Leaders' Initiative. In my interview, I shared about starting the Esther Project. Our name was inspired by the young girl in the Bible who trusted God and went from a nobody to a big player in God's plan. We discipled young girls who had been disadvantaged, often through early marriage, lack of education, or disability. By helping them access school or learn a trade, we empowered them to know their identity in Christ and live out their potential.

I told them about Wilta, a member of the Esther Project. We shared a middle name as well as similar symptoms and experiences. She reached out to me from Bafut, her village, where she had been sent to live with her grandmother. Her parents lived in the city. Wilta's grandmother sought treatment for Wilta's disability but never neglected her granddaughter's education. For many years, she carried her on her back to and from school, until the grandmother grew too old and frail. When Wilta reached out to me, she was demurely hoping for a better life in the future, although she was not quite sure how. I mentored her and contributed toward her school fees so she could continue her education.

To my surprise, my application was accepted! I was excited at the prospect of finally setting foot in America – the land of possibilities I had only been privileged to see through books and movies. Moving home had not been the dead end I had feared after all, but a stepping stone to my next adventure.

The weeks leading up to the departure were frantic, involving several trips from Bamenda to the main office in Yaoundé to get my passport renewed in time. My sister, Britha, after her wedding the year before, was expecting a baby. My parents and Britha moved in with me so my parents could assist in her delivery and me in my travelling preparations. The evenings were festive as we sat together, sharing ideas on what the journey was going to be like. The novelty of this experience for my family was evident in their questions about how I was going to cope.

"What if you will not be able to eat the 'white man's food' for all this while?" one of my brothers asked. We all laughed.

I replied, "Well, it will help me lose weight and I will make sure I carry enough food with me." A heated argument followed about whether food was allowed on planes at all.

Truthfully, I was afraid of taking into the skies in a wheelchair. At this time, I was more dependent than ever. To get into and out of cars, I had to be carried from the wheelchair. I couldn't imagine this working the same way for an aeroplane, let alone with strangers in another culture.

My greatest concern, though, was how I could be in America for over three months without the assistance of one or more members of my family for the first time. It was almost impossible for me to muster up the courage to go to a faraway land without family to fall back on.

I wrote to the YALI team, explaining that with the nature of my disability I could not travel alone. Could I bring a family member as an assistant? My request was seemingly out of the norms of the US embassy. After many email exchanges, it seemed I would have to turn down the opportunity to travel to America for the first time.

Finally, the head of the cohort got in touch. Thanks to her advocacy, my sister Tewah was allowed to come to America with me.

After an almost eight-hour road trip from my hometown, we arrived at the airport. For the day of our trip, I had donned blue denim trousers bought from the Bamenda Main Market, a blue blazer made from African print, and blue sandals prepared for this occasion. My sister also dressed in tailor-made African-print clothes.

At the counter, the agent called up someone supposedly trained to handle cases of wheelchair travellers like me. I was grateful we were flying with Air France; the other airlines didn't offer assistance. The assistant took control of my manual chair. There were a few flights of steps between the check-in area and the plane. It was challenging, but we managed with some help from other airport workers.

My sister and I were the first to board the plane. When we reached the door of the plane, my wheelchair could go no further. An aisle chair, which is a slimmer wheelchair designed to fit between the seats, quelled my worries about how to travel as a quadriplegic.

"Tewah, come and hold me from behind so he can hold my legs and you lift." She moved to grab me under the arms just like she had done countless times before. The assistant lifted my legs.

Once I was seated, they rolled the aisle chair backwards down the aisle to my seat, then transferred me again to the plane seat. While it was heartwarming to receive the pampering of the plane crew, I could tell from their frantic glances and hushed whispers that it was not every day they received a passenger who flew in a wheelchair. Tewah and I snapped a picture. It was not every day we travelled by plane either!

My excitement kept me awake for all 13 hours of travel from Douala, Cameroon, through Charles de Gaulle Airport in Paris, and on to San Francisco. It was a long and exhausting trip, but I could hardly believe this was happening.

As the plane lifted off, my heart leapt as if this moment stood for more than an aircraft transitioning from taxiing to flying in the air. I thought of the vivacious Evelyn Afombom and the resilient Wilta Bih. I was carrying their stories with me across the ocean. We might have disabilities, but maybe the sky didn't have to be the limit.

The first few days in America I was a mix of emotions. On the one hand, I was elated to see places I had read about or heard of in the news. I got to meet and learn from people coming from diverse backgrounds. On the other, it was a struggle to adapt to a new place. When people back home asked how I liked the food, I replied that everything was much too sweet.

Old friends who were familiar with both of our cultures advised us on how to navigate the treacherous food and other basics of this world. They bought and mailed us some of the things we needed.

I called Sara Tanner, whom I had translated for when she came to Cameroon, and she helped me to make sense of the American way of life. I recalled how she had ended up in Cameroon. When she was 19, a missionary visited her church, which ignited a passion for the lost in her. Many years later, Sara found a long-lost letter that the missionary had sent her from Cameroon. It rekindled her desire to serve God in Cameroon. Now, here I was crossing cultures to visit her homeland.

Two days into my stay in Berkeley, I was introduced to my first power chair. The programme coordinator had rented it for my stay. My sister transferred me into the fancy Jazzy power chair while the technicians and some staff watched on nervously.

At first, I was fearful. I imagined moving from a manual to a power chair would be like learning to drive a car. It was reassuring to see that sitting in this wasn't too different from the manual chair. I practised on the lowest speed setting. By the end of the day, I was able to roll myself back to our living quarters at the International House. I kept it on the lowest speed for the next few days, but the more I rolled, the faster and more confident I got.

Much like my tricycle of many years before, this power chair gave me newfound freedom that stirred my love for adventure. I was out and about every chance I got, with or without my sister. It amazed me that I could take off for walks or visiting on my own.

Drivers would stop to let me cross the road without hurrying me along or making comments. Bus passengers would give up their seats every time I or another wheelchair user entered the bus. One bus driver came out of the bus to explain to me why she could not take me on board because her ramp had a mechanical failure. I hoped someday we would see such positive changes back home.

We settled into a routine of daily interactions with various speakers at The Goldman School of Public Policy. On the days that we were not seated in class, our group of 26 was bussed out to visit some of the marvels of the Bay Area and Silicon Valley: many museums, national parks, the state capital in Sacramento, and even a baseball match. Each visit was a joyful experience, immersing us deeper into American ways. When we were given a tour of the Google headquarters and received at the Oracle Center, we were in awe at being on these premises of companies we had only heard of. The expansive stretch of both headquarters left me wondering how finite minds could conceive such grandeur. *And here I had thought leaving Yaoundé was limiting my horizons!*

After six weeks, we were to spend the next eight weeks of our fellowship experience in Washington DC. Before the trip to DC, the friends in my cohort started raising money to buy a power chair to take along. They could not raise enough, so another wheelchair was rented for me in DC.

We took the seed money and continued fundraising for a wheelchair that I could take home. Issa Nyaphagha, who had initially told me about YALI, had previously made a video of me in Cameroon in the old wheelchair. He came together with his friends and raised what was needed to get a power chair that I could take back home to Cameroon.

I was thrilled that I was going to be carrying my newfound freedom from America back to Cameroon. I was accustomed to constant stares whenever I hit the streets of my hometown, Bamenda or other places back home in my manual wheelchair. I couldn't wait to see what the reactions would be to me cruising along by myself in this power chair.

CHAPTER 28

Joni

When I got to Washington DC, Sara Tanner visited me. She knew what impact Joni Eareckson Tada had made on my story and decided it was time to make my long-cherished dream come true. I had no idea how it could be possible, but she contacted Joni's assistant to set up a visit. Then, she graciously bought plane tickets for my sister and me.

Through the kindness of this little saint and a series of inexplicable circumstances, in answer to many a night of whispered prayers and many unanswered letters, the Lord brought me to California. I was going to meet Joni Eareckson Tada, the lady whose story had changed my life.

When I arrived at the hotel in Los Angeles, I was fuzzy-headed and operating on adrenaline. I hadn't slept for 48 hours, due to a whole night of hair plaiting and my excitement to finally fulfil my dream.

"How may I help you?" asked the smiling receptionist.

"I reserved a room here a few days ago."

"What's your last name please?"

"Muluh, M-U-L . . ."

"Got it. Your room is ready, Ma'am."

"Is it an ADA room?" He looked startled, so I restated my question. "Is it handicapped accessible?" I had come to learn while I was in America that a law enacted in 1990 provided for public areas to be accessible to people with disabilities. Referred to as the Americans with Disabilities Act, or ADA for short, it ensured that people with disabilities had their rights respected. I was determined to take every opportunity this law offered while my stay lasted.

I watched with elation as the concierge scurried around, rallying his team to get the room ready. Someone who had been to America had told me before I came that I would be treated as royalty here. And yes, this was as close to regal as I could feel.

September 15. I had inscribed the date in my mental notebook ever since Lisa, Joni's assistant had confirmed my appointment. That morning, we woke early. Our appointment was not until 2 p.m., but I urged my sister to get me ready, despite knowing she was tired from the previous few days.

The hotel was within walking distance of the Joni and Friends International Disability Center. I sped ahead of Tewah, looking for a sign with Joni's insignia, which I had come to recognize over the years. Since acquiring a power chair, I had regained my leadership position as the older sister that I had enjoyed when we were much younger. When people saw me being pushed in a wheelchair, they would tend to speak to the person assisting me as if I wasn't there. But with a power chair, I could zoom ahead of my sister so people would talk to me first. I could make my presence felt in a new way.

The interior of the Center was more sophisticated than the simple outside suggested. It was an ultra-modern building with a distinctive architectural design. The symbol of the cross greeted us as we made our entrance. Clear water emerged from beneath the cross, running over the words of the beautiful verse from Amos 5:24, "But let justice roll on like a river, righteousness like a never-failing stream!"

At my request, the receptionist showed us the chapel. I hurried ahead of my sister because I intended to raise my altar of thanks to God here. As I got in, I was filled with a real sense of awe, not at the splendour of the tiny chapel, but at memories of God's faithfulness through the years. He had brought me so far, from the dusty, crammed classroom of my high school days where I first read Joni's story all the way to Southern California where Joni, the person, lived. I opened the Bible at the front of the chapel, but my eyes were too blurred with tears to read it. I looked over to read the verse inscribed on the wall: "Lord, our Lord, how majestic is your name in all the earth!" (Psalm 8:1).

"Lord, forgive me. I'm sorry I have doubted you so many times, even when you called on me to trust you. Thank you, Lord. Help me to trust you going forward." Unable to raise my hands, I used my shoulder to pat my wet eyes before my sister arrived.

We continued our tour of the International Disability Center, playing for time. Everything here was a model of a wheelchair-accessible environment. We moved up the ramp to the fifth floor to Joni's office where our meeting was scheduled.

I looked at my watch, a stylish lady watch that my host had offered me and my sister the day before. It was 2 p.m.

A woman emerged from an adjoining room – Lisa. She gave me a warm hug and welcomed us officially. She apologized, explaining that Joni was finishing her lunch. My nerves cracked again. In the meantime, Bryan, the global ministry director of Joni and Friends, engaged me and my sister in small talk.

"Hello." I heard her voice echo from behind me. I recognized it from the radio programmes I had listened to sometime before. Joni wheeled to my side.

"Oh my God, oh my God, oh my God!" I couldn't contain my exhilaration. I was seeing Joni Eareckson Tada, whose life story had become so intertwined with mine, though we were born thousands of kilometres and many years apart. I had imagined countless times what I would say when I met her the first time, either on this side of eternity or in heaven. The latter had seemed more feasible given my reality, but God had proven to me time and time again that my plans were not his.

Joni looked much more youthful than I had imagined her to be at over 60. Her cropped hair gave her a girlish demeanour, but subtle makeup complimented her looks. She had on an animal-print blouse with elbow-length sleeves, leaving room for her hand splints to be seen. I noted her manicured nails and well-tailored black pants. I had been made to sometimes feel that there was no point in taking care of paralyzed limbs and inactive hands, but I was glad to share the same opinion as Joni.

My sister took a few clicks as a professional photographer immortalized our meeting. Joni led us back into her office for a chit-chat before proceeding.

"So, Hilda how long have you been around the Los Angeles area?"

"Only since yesterday, Joni. We flew in from DC yesterday afternoon." My voice still shivered from the excitement I felt.

"You went through a lot of trouble just to come see me."

I nodded. My eyes were tearing up. "It was worth it. Words can hardly tell how much this moment means to me." I was getting emotional again.

She noticed and turned to my sister, "So you have been with her all this while?"

"Yes, I have," Tewah answered timidly.

"Thank you for your sacrifice." She turned to me again, "Your sister reminds me of the sacrifice my sisters made for me, especially in the years after my accident."

She had hit a mutual soft spot. I nodded again. We both sniffed and blinked away our tears before she continued, "Tell me about the rest of your family. Are both of your parents alive? Do they live in Cameroon too?" She went on with a barrage of questions.

As she enquired about our parents, she wheeled quickly to the other side of the room. She asked an assistant to grab a handful of her books for our parents, my sister, and me. Joni signed the books for us with the pen held in her mouth. I was overjoyed.

Next, she showed us her art studio, where she spent many an hour. She had become famous for painting with her mouth, and we saw her many tooth-marked brushes and easel. She explained how some pencils had to be taped to others and foam attached to achieve a particular effect. She also gave us one of her paintings to take home.

I was fascinated to see a red pair of sports shoes. She informed us that they were a gift from some parents who had attended her family retreat. She planned to wear the shoes to her funeral. Joni's spirited outlook confirmed the impression I had long held of her.

We recorded my story for her radio programme before singing a hymn together: "Amazing Grace". What better hymn to celebrate the triumph over adversity in both our lives, we who had not only been saved by God's amazing grace but had been called to depend on grace at every moment of the journey? As we got to the third verse, my favourite, I harmonized under Joni's commanding voice:

Through many dangers, toils and snares,
I have already come,
'Twas grace that brought me safe thus far
And grace will lead me home.

The final verse took my mind to scenes of heaven. A smile formed on my lips as I pictured Joni, myself, and countless others, skipping on the streets of gold. "When we've been there, ten thousand years" – our earthly vessels and burdens a distant memory away as we revel in the glory of the King – "bright shining as the sun" – praising and giving glory to the one who gave our lives meaning through his amazing grace – "we've no less days to sing God's praise than when we first begun."

It was well worth living for this!

The final few days spent in Washington DC, after we returned from California, went by like a wind. An airline strike prolonging our stay by a few days did little to dampen my enthusiasm to return home.

We left the hotel for the airport so early that the neon lights waved us goodbye. My sister was not coming along with me on this flight.

I prayed as we took off. As I opened my eyes, snacks were being served by two beautiful East African flight attendants. I stared down at my little airline table with its water and biscuits. I had no idea how I was going to feed myself.

This was the first time in a long time that I found myself with no one to help feed me or give me a drink. The man sitting next to me asked if he could help. I shook my head, closing my eyes to hide my burning tears. I hated to cry in public.

In my struggle to accept my weakening body, there are rare moments when I have deeply, sincerely prayed that God will grant me some use of my hands, even if temporarily. This was one of them. My uncontrollable tears drew the attention of the flight crew. They tried to no avail to comfort me. I prayed for the embarrassing tears to go away, but they would not.

Eventually, when I stopped crying, I was left with a streaked face and running nose that I also could do little about. I realized I was exhausted from the previous sleepless nights. I felt helpless and terribly lonely without my sister, who had been my constant companion for the past God knows how long. I had sunk down into a pool of self-pity. I called on Jesus to encircle me with his comforting embrace, then drifted to sleep.

A gentle touch on my right shoulder woke me. A middle-aged passenger had stooped to speak close to my ear. "Sister." Her voice was kind, her accent was thickly East African. "Do you like to pray?"

I was taken aback by her out-of-the-blue question and stuttered, searching for an answer in my mind.

She rested a reassuring hand on my shoulder. "I pray in the name of Jesus Christ."

"Of course," I mumbled.

She straightened up, turned around, and spoke in a language I didn't understand. Before I knew it, I was surrounded by an army of believers in the Lord Jesus Christ. They held my hands, surrounded me, and prayed the sweetest prayer I ever took part in. Despite the stares of other passengers, I felt the comforting presence of my Lord as they lifted me up before the throne of grace. At the "Amen", the entire group gave me hugs before returning to their seats.

I thanked God for answering the prayer I had uttered earlier. Here, more than 12 kilometres or 40,000 feet above the ground, God had used a group of praying Christians in the air to prove to me that he was holding me.

As I considered the remaining part of my long, arduous, uncertain journey, I felt confident that God was greater than all the daunting complexities of my life. I knew with firm assurance that:

Grace hath brought me safe thus far,
And Grace will lead me home.

Radio is fun – an outdoor broadcast in Bamenda

2014 with Tewah, my first flight

Meeting Joni Eareckson Tada

With Elvis, receiving an award in Atlanta, GA in 2015

Afterword

A few years have gone by since I wrote the last words of *The Girl with Special Shoes*. I have continued to walk through many open doors and watch God do amazing things in my life and even use my story in the lives of others around me.

Most nights, after I'm tucked into bed with the lights turned off, I look at the silhouette of my wheelchair sitting lonely in the dark corner of the room and it makes me giggle. Looking back at the thoughts I used to have about wheelchairs, I'm amused at how the divine sense of humour continues to play out in my story. The wheelchair I once considered the worst instrument of torture has turned out to be the greatest vessel of blessing. I am grateful that God has his ways which, although never what I wish for, are meant to mould me into a vessel that he can use.

God is still writing my story. As my body continues to weaken, at times I fear what lies ahead. In my usual impatience, I want to peer ahead to know what is in store. All I see is a promise of grace that abounds as weakness grows. Grace is certainly a wave I can ride on fearlessly to discover new shores.

I hear many stories of triumph over disability in my community, my country, and beyond. I rejoice to see some progress being made to change the harmful perceptions about disability that previously condemned some people in the shadows for good. I have come to see that there is no greater power than the good news of Jesus to free souls held captive by ignorance and harmful beliefs in this broken world. Unfortunately, many people still lack access to this great news.

Recently, I learned about a child of a distant cousin, severely disabled from birth, born to parents with little means to take her to a hospital. She was taken to a renowned witch doctor who gave a prescription that would return her to the spirit world and free her parents of this burden. My mother learned of the incident a few days after the child had been killed and told me.

Words can hardly express how heartbroken I was to hear of this practice, which I believed was obsolete, and to hear of it so close to home. Her story could have been my story, yet, by some miracle, I am living and breathing. Her story and others that I come across as I am exposed to other cultures are harsh reminders that brokenness and despair are everywhere.

The most vulnerable people in society shouldn't be shackled in the shadows. God has imprinted his image on us; we reflect something about who he is to the world. People with disabilities and others often peer into the future and wonder if we should keep going. Some people find themselves in such dark tunnels they can't find a way out. Let's reignite the light and shine the pathway of hope for each other. God has given us potential, has plans for us to flourish and live into our purpose. No one is a burden; we can all bless others. We can be all confident that we are part of a bigger story, and it ends in ultimate victory where all broken bodies will be restored.

God is rewriting our own happy endings, one story at a time.

Acknowledgements

My journey in life has been enriched so much and by so many people that it would take another book to write down each name. I'm humbled and grateful to the entire village that made this life an adventure and this book possible.

Thank you to my parents, whose relentless and selfless love gives me a glimpse of what the everlasting love of my heavenly Father looks like.

To my siblings and extended family, thank you for bearing me on your strong backs and never getting weary of caring for me. You have shown me that love and sacrifice can enable one to endure the most trying times.

To my friends and siblings in the faith, your prayers and constant encouragement to grow in grace give me hope, pointing to the light that leads home.

I am grateful to my local church at The Well for the joy of being a member of the body of Christ and for their commitment to seeing me grow as a vessel that can be useful to the Lord.

To Joni and Friends, I'm grateful that you blazed a trail, holding out the light of Christ so I and others could see and follow.

Thank you to all teachers who kept me on the path of life and the pursuit of knowledge. Thanks to you, I was able to see a world of wonders beyond my walls and reach for it.

I owe a debt of gratitude to Sister Petra and the Franciscan Nuns in SAJOCAH who took in me and other children like me when nobody else wanted us.

To the Oasis team, thank you for guiding me through the daunting process of publishing and making sure the message of hope in Jesus shared in this book reaches further and wider than I could have done on my own.

If you're holding this book in your hand or reading my story, then you are the reason it was written. You are a part of my story – thank you and God bless.

You may feel weakness is blocking your path. But often, it's the route God has planned.

Hilda has seen God's power and ability in her pain and disability. She is passionate about using her story to let the light of Christ shine through so others can come to know him. She wants to uplift others with the hope she has found.

If you're looking for:

- An inspirational speaker for your event
- Encouragement and awareness around disability
- How you can support needs in Cameroon

Visit HildaBih.com

OASIS
INTERNATIONAL
PUBLISHING

oasisinternationalpublishing.com

Oasis will become the first publisher capable of placing a book or Bible in every Christian reader's hand in Africa.
Go to oasisinternationalpublishing.com to learn more.

THE DISCIPLER'S TOOLKIT
George M. Mutuku and Mark A. Olander
The churches in Sub-Saharan Africa are growing numerically, primarily through evangelism. But evangelism is only the beginning of the disciple making process. This book takes people step by step from evangelism to establishing new believers in the faith, equipping them in spiritual disciplines and gifts, and sending them out to engage the world with the gospel.

ESSENTIAL LEADERSHIP LESSONS
Richard J. Gehman
Essential Leadership Lessons covers topics of leadership essentials, humility, love, holiness, attributes, management skills, and common issues. While the context and application of these leadership lessons were created with the people of Africa in mind, the principles of Christian leadership are the same everywhere, for everyone, on all continents.

STAND UP FOR THE GOSPEL
Emmanuel Kwasi Amoafo
This book is a timely wake-up call about what is happening in many of our churches today. It will equip you to defend our timeless faith. In the midst of counterfeits, rediscover the refreshing truths of God's Word, and the glorious, life-transforming gospel of Jesus Christ.

I ONCE WAS DEAD
Cedric Kanana with Benjamin Fischer
This book's riveting, action-packed plot has one central message shining through: Jesus is stronger than death, than addiction, than Islam, than curses. Trust Jesus alone! The miracles recorded in *I Once Was Dead* echo the book of Acts and give all glory to God – whether healing, deliverance, resurrection, protection from threats, or hearing God's voice.

THE ESSENTIAL GUIDE TO THE BIBLE AND CHRISTIANITY
John Jusu and Matthew Elliott
Situating each book of the Bible in the context of the whole Bible clarifies truths that are less clear when taken out of context. This guide will help you understand, from a biblical perspective, how the visible world connects with the realities of the unseen world surrounding us.

THE SISTERHOOD SECRET
Levina Mulandi
In this book, Dr Mulandi shows how discipling is more than Bible study or a church program. She shares how she empowers any woman to mentor younger women, guiding them to understand their identity, discern the purpose of their lives, and be transformed to be more like Christ.

HAPPILY WHENEVER AFTER
Bookie Adekanye
Candid and kind, Bookie Adekanye reminds you of God's overwhelming love for you. No matter how society labels you, God says you belong to him. You're invited to heal from past scars and be your confident, courageous self. The God of the Bible used single ladies to deliver and save, and he definitely has a plan for you.

BAESICS
Ernest Wamboye with Waturi Wamboye
In *Baesics*, Ernest and Waturi Wamboye give no-nonsense advice on how to build a fulfilling love life and marriage. Young adults in African cities feel marriage is priority but are often unprepared. *Baesics* addresses the relationship dilemmas many young adults are facing today from a Christian point of view.

GETTING MARRIED?
Chao Tsuma Wanje and James Wanje
Written as a friendly and light-hearted conversation, this book is perfect for you and your fiancé(e) to read and discuss together. Drawing from timeless wisdom and real-life examples, this husband-and-wife team helps couples to resolve conflicts before they explode.

THE DIVORCE DILEMMA
Ron Misiko & Ray Motsi
The authors share their experiences as pastors and as married people, as well as their areas of expertise in the legal system and Bible scholarship. From their different African contexts, they explain how to navigate the challenges we face today with biblical and practical solutions for divorce care in African churches.

OASIS INTERNATIONAL PUBLISHING

oasisinternationalpublishing.com

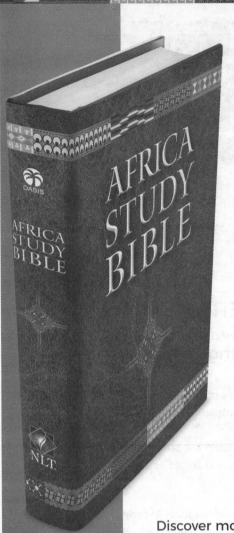

AFRICA STUDY BIBLE, NLT
God's Word Through African Eyes

The *Africa Study Bible* is the most ethnically-diverse, single-volume, biblical resource to date. Written by 350 contributors from 50 countries, it includes the Holy Bible: New Living Translation, and more than 2,600 features that illuminate the truth of Scripture with a unique, African perspective.

The *Africa Study Bible* is a monumental study Bible, with notes by scholars and pastors in Africa who see the critical need to make Scripture relevant to our everyday lives. It's an all-in-one course in biblical content, theology, history, and culture.

"The **Africa Study Bible** *is a model of contextualized engagement of the Scriptures, with notes written by Africans, written for Africans, and answers Bible questions asked in African cultural contexts. It's a great encouragement to me to see such a resource available and I recommend it widely!"*
- Dr Ed Stetzer, Executive Director of the BILLY GRAHAM CENTER

Discover more at *africastudybible.com*

DOWNLOAD THE
AFRICA STUDY BIBLE APP

The Africa Study Bible app is now on the Tecarta Bible App, the world's best study Bible app which is available to download on Google Play Store and Apple App Store.

SATISFYING AFRICA'S THIRST FOR GOD'S WORD

OASIS INTERNATIONAL
is devoted to growing discipleship through publishing African voices.

Engaging Africa's most influential,
most relevant, and best communicators for the sake of the gospel.

Creating contextual content that meets the specific needs of Africa, has
the power to transform individuals and societies, and gives the church
in Africa a global voice.

Cultivating local and global partnerships in order to publish
and distribute high-quality books and Bibles.

Visit **oasisinternational.com** to learn more about our vision;
for Africa to equip its own leaders to impact the global church.

oasisinternational.com   oasisinternationalpublishing.com   godswordforafrica.com